Dimes Square and Other Plays

Dimes Square
and Other Plays

Matthew Gasda

Foreword by Christian Lorentzen

APPLAUSE
THEATRE & CINEMA BOOKS

Essex, Connecticut

APPLAUSE
THEATRE & CINEMA BOOKS

An imprint of Globe Pequot, the trade division of
The Rowman & Littlefield Publishing Group, Inc.
4501 Forbes Blvd., Ste. 200
Lanham, MD 20706
www.rowman.com

Distributed by NATIONAL BOOK NETWORK

Library of Congress Cataloging-in-Publication Data

Names: Gasda, Matthew, author. | Lorentzen, Christian, writer of foreword.
Title: Dimes Square and other plays / Matthew Gasda ; foreword by Christian Lorentzen.
Description: Essex, Connecticut : Applause Theatre & Cinema Books, [2023] |
  Summary: "This collection contains the plays Dimes Square, Quartet, Berlin Story, and Minotaur by dramatist Matthew Gasda, following his meteoric rise in New York's downtown scene" —Provided by publisher.
Identifiers: LCCN 2022058009 (print) | LCCN 2022058010 (ebook) | ISBN 9781493075713 (paperback ; alk. paper) | ISBN 9781493075720 (epub)
Subjects: LCGFT: Drama.
Classification: LCC PS3607.A7845 D56 2023 (print) | LCC PS3607.A7845 (ebook) | DDC 812/.6—dc23/eng/20221220
LC record available at https://lccn.loc.gov/2022058009
LC ebook record available at https://lccn.loc.gov/2022058010

♾️™ The paper used in this publication meets the minimum requirements of American National Standard for Information Sciences—Permanence of Paper for Printed Library Materials, ANSI/NISO Z39.48-1992.

Contents

Foreword

by Christian Lorentzen

It would be absurd to say that we are living in a golden age of the underground arts in America. The last half century has seen the consolidation of book publishing under five, perhaps soon to be four, international corporations. Independent film, which was flourishing as recently as two decades ago, has now become a pendant on a rotating set of franchise pictures screened at multiplexes that are shuttered week after week. Television and popular music are dominated by corporate streaming services that distribute their product by algorithm. Broadway is captive to the jukebox musical, the star-driven revival, and productions that generate hype from topicality.

Yet the same technologies and material conditions that have brought about this scenario cannot help but cause the rise of something like its opposite. Matthew Gasda, a young writer living in New York City after the turn of the millennium and making a living as writers often have—by teaching, tutoring, coaching debate, and so on—seemed to realize this. For several years he has been writing plays and putting them on in rooms around the city, marshaling casts of trained and amateur performers, drawing audiences through a combination of email blasts and old-fashioned word of mouth. In short, he has hustled, to find spaces, to find talent, sometimes even to find chairs.

I met Gasda at a party in a backyard in Brooklyn in June of 2021. It was a few months after the vaccines became available and people were getting out again after months of being shut in or bound to wholesome outdoor activities. (Gasda, it turned out, had already been getting people out, putting on plays in parks.) It turned out we already knew each other, in a way. We had been messaging over Twitter, where he went by the handle Novalis, and I had been subscribing to the newsletter he put out under the same name. He invited me to one of his plays, *Quartet*. The experience, on a Sunday evening at a loft in Soho, was bracing: writing that was thoroughly contemporary but unbound by current pieties; energetic comic performances by young actors putting themselves on the line; and above all an intimate human scale to the production. After the show, when Gasda told me the next play he was working on was called *Dimes Square*, I asked if I could audition.

Dimes Square is the slang name for a corner in Manhattan where Canal Street meets Essex Street and the Lower East Side shades into Chinatown, near the East Broadway subway stop on the F line. (A restaurant called Dimes is there, and "dimes" is slang for models who are "10s," and of course there's the pun on Times Square.) In the years just before the pandemic, the zone had become for many, myself and Gasda included, the last refuge in a downtown that had become hopelessly touristic, overrun by New York University, and generally uncool, or at least not as much fun as it used to be. Gasda's play takes place in a loft where a set of young people and a couple of has-beens—writers, filmmakers, an editor, an artist, an actress, a fashion-world person—have it out about their ambitions, frustrations, and rivalries over copious amounts of alcohol, tobacco, and various powders. There are references to the neighborhood—the restaurant Kiki's, the Metrograph cinema, the bars Clandestino and 169—as well as to recent and hardly permanent phenomena like Netflix, Instagram, and dating apps, but the play's themes are timeless: ambition, envy, ostracism, hedonism, insecurity, lust, heartbreak, and what it means to be an artist.

In a town where people had grown tired and bored by the corporate culture being streamed into the homes where they had literally been quarantined (also the sort of culture some of the characters in *Dimes Square* aspire to create), the play struck a nerve, our shows sold out, we got our pictures in *The New York Times*, and many think pieces were launched— in magazines, on Substack, and in cul-de-sacs of the internet even more obscure. After a while, the discourse died down—it had briefly been enflamed by the mistaken notion that the play and the scene it depicted were genuinely new, rather than a fresh acting-out and living-out of perennial human foibles—but the crowds kept coming, as over the summer and autumn of 2022, Gasda revived his earlier plays *Minotaur* and *Quartet* and premiered *Berlin Story*.

These are not plays that offer answers, takes, or mere supplements to the churning river of thoughtlings, idealets, and other mental debris that trickle minute by minute across our screens. They are the result of Gasda's social observations and solitary contemplations, followed by months of revisions undertaken in collaboration with actors and other interlocutors in workshop readings as he prepares his plays for production. Gasda has a classical sensibility, and the reader will discover that these plays are in dialogue with recognizable traditions and with each other. The bohemians of *Dimes Square* have their foils among the fractured family of *Minotaur*; the cynical characters of *Berlin Story* practice a form of deliberate dissipation that the bourgeois couples of *Quartet* are doing their best not to fall into accidentally.

I will stop before I fall into the habits of a critic making facile comparisons (watch out for the names of Gaddis, Joyce, Chekhov, Isherwood) or the actor dishing inside dope (certain versions of *Berlin Story* involved a lot of spitting). Now that they are between covers and not just being performed in rooms in Manhattan and Brooklyn, these plays of Gasda's are yours to interpret as you will, whether in solitude or collaborative performance. Some of the behaviors and attitudes enacted and expressed by the characters in these pages—incest, adultery, careerism, cynicism, intoxication, pornography, war tourism—belie the commitment brought to these works by their author and his initial collaborators. They are, in the slang of Rosie from *Dimes Square*, "based." The plays' conception has been, and their further contemplation and execution, should be entirely otherwise.

Dimes Square

"What's any artist, but the dregs of his work? The human shambles that follows it around. What's left of the man when the work's done but a shambles of apology."

—William Gaddis, *The Recognitions*

Dimes Square premiered at Ty's Loft in Greenpoint, Brooklyn in February of 2022 with the following cast:

Iris: Agnes Enkhtamir
Nate: Jordan Lester
Stefan: Maximilian Macdonald
Klay: Bijan Stephen
Ashley: Helena Dreyer
Terry: Connor Hall
Olivia: Fernanda Amis
Bora: Eunji Lim
Rosie: Cassidy Grady
Chris: Bob Laine
Dave: Christian Lorentzen

Directed by Matthew Gasda
Dramaturg Danielle Carr
Stage Managed by Patrick Callahan
Produced by Matthew Gasda and Gabrielle Bluestone

Cast of Characters:

Iris: MFA poet, 25
Klay: journo dude, 30
Nate: indie musician, 28
Stefan: writer, 28
Ashley: college student, 19
Terry: filmmaker, 30
Rosie: scene girl, artist, 26
Bora: cinematographer, 30
Dave: novelist, 45

Chris: editor, 55
Olivia: fashionista, 24

Setting:

An apartment in Chinatown. Foucault stacks on the floor, empty box of Marlboros and a copy of the *Drunken Canal* on the table. A little dirty.

One

Iris and Nate sit smoking in someone else's apartment.

IRIS

I've met her six times now and every single time she says 'nice to meet you . . . and I'm like . . . bitch, I've met you . . . many, many times . . . '

NATE

We are living through the dumbest time in human history.

IRIS

How many times do I have to share my drugs with you before you recognize me as human?

NATE

Apparently more than several.

IRIS

I wish to be euthanized.

NATE

Go for it.

IRIS

Can you help?

NATE

That's not really my kink.

IRIS

I don't know why people care that we're fucking. Why is it such a topic?

NATE

We're not even that interesting.

IRIS

Compared to all the cuffed and bored couples we know we are—

NATE

I guess.

IRIS

It gets tiresome having to pretend that everyone is like doing SO well and is SO happy in their relationship and having to validate their retarded emotions all the time. Should we fuck like right now?

NATE

They're gonna be back in like ninety seconds.

IRIS

So? It'd be fun.

NATE

I'm sorry about the other night by the way . . .

IRIS

Stop apologizing; it's over.

NATE

I was sloppy—

IRIS

Oh well—

NATE

I feel guilty—

IRIS

You don't need my permission. Do whatever you want. Did you see what Eva tweeted?

NATE

Is it more sad girl shit?

IRIS

She thinks your album is *literally* about her.

NATE

Uh, no, it's literally not about anyone.

IRIS

Ok, tell her that.

NATE

Not worth the effort.

IRIS

You shouldn't let people form these fantasies about you; like haven't you learned your lesson?

NATE

Let's not go there . . .

IRIS

As you wish. Can I tell you something that might sound like an invitation, but is in fact a cry for help?

NATE

Go for it.

IRIS

I own a strap on. However, I don't use it; I like to dress up in it and watch myself in the mirror. It really turns me on. So . . . then I just take it off and masturbate.

NATE

Dope.

IRIS

I've never told anyone that.

NATE

That's for the best.

IRIS

Sure.

NATE

Whenever you don't make eye-contact, you're having negative thoughts.

IRIS

I'm planning to find someone else soon, just FYI.

NATE

Figured.

IRIS

So enjoy me while you have me baby. . . . What?

NATE

I don't think you realize . . .

IRIS

What?

IRIS	NATE
	Iris you're a lifeline . . .
Oh not this again—	
	in more ways than one . . .
please—	

IRIS

Nate we need to be clear on a
few things . . .

I can't be on call for you every time
you have an emotional breakdown,
no matter how warranted those
breakdowns are—

it's too much—

it's . . .

not my fault what happened to
you—at all—and like

Nate—

When was the last time you were
with someone who wasn't your
fucking fan?

NATE
I feel selfish for even saying this;
it feels pathetic. . . .

Like what?

That I'm fucking in love with you?

fuck-

ing-

in love.

L

O

V

E

Iris

I'd even let you peg me with
your vanity dick—

NATE
    No idea.

IRIS
    Right.

NATE
    I dunno if I can ever forgive you for choosing to be with me without really being with
    me.

IRIS
    Is it your intent, sir, to make me cry?

NATE
    I'm not sure what my intention is.

IRIS

Because I'm on the verge. . . .

NATE

Iris. My head hurts. My chest hurts. I spent all day swiping to find a backup plan for you on dating apps, just swiping and swiping. But . . . I'm terrified of giving anyone my full name in case they Google me. Plus I don't want to actually meet anyone else. I would stop everything I'm doing just to be around you a little longer; I'm counting down the motherfucking days until you ghost me. Like. It's wild how much this open-relationship or secret relationship or unlabeled relationship is occupying my mental space. I just feel like I'm in such a weakened state, like a dying animal covered in flies. . . . I'm so full of resentment and love at the same time and it makes no sense. None. . . . Last night, during the storm, I just sat in my apartment listening to Sonic Youth records and I felt like a fucking teenager . . .

Enter Stefan, Ashley, and Klay.

NATE

Yo.

KLAY

We got booze.

IRIS

You guys took forever.

STEFAN

It took forever to find a place that sold Fernet.

NATE

Sorry.

IRIS

I don't think we've met before; what's your name?

ASHLEY

Ashley.

IRIS

Iris.

ASHLEY

Nice to meet you.

IRIS

Enchanté.

STEFAN
> What's up Iris?

IRIS
> Nothing.

STEFAN
> Do you want some Fernet?

IRIS
> No, that stuff tastes like mouthwash.

NATE
> It's good; you just gotta get used to it.

ASHLEY
> I'll try some . . .

STEFAN
> Do you want a beer?

IRIS
> Yeah I'll have a beer.

ASHLEY
> I've realized lately that I have no impulse control.

KLAY
> You don't need it.

STEFAN
> Why don't you pour me half of that Ashley—

ASHLEY
> Ok, daddy, here ya go.

IRIS
> I read your novel Stefan—

STEFAN
> Did you like it?

IRIS
> It was fun . . .

STEFAN
> Fun.

IRIS
> Mhmm.

STEFAN
> You hated it—

IRIS	ASHLEY
No!	
Lies!	He's a touchy boy . . .
Don't twist my words . . .	

STEFAN
Fun.

IRIS
Dude, you just sold the rights to Netflix.

STEFAN
What's your point?

IRIS
My point is: you don't need my approval.

STEFAN
I guess not.

KLAY
That's so dope about the show though.

STEFAN
Thanks.

KLAY
Are you guys looking for writers?

STEFAN
I mean, I can pass your name along to the show-runners for sure.

KLAY
Damn, really?

STEFAN
For sure. Let's do coffee this week; we can talk about it.

KLAY
I'm down. Thank you so much. Wow.

STEFAN
Any time.

NATE
Did you guys see Terry's film?

STEFAN
It's alright.

KLAY

He's kind of a brilliant.

STEFAN

Let's not get carried away.

NATE

I don't even like movies very much and I think it's very fucking good.

KLAY

Even Dave gave it a begrudging thumb slightly north of sideways.

STEFAN

Dave's got no braincells left.

KLAY

I'm actually writing about Terry for Vice.

IRIS	STEFAN
Is that self parody or a real thing?	Good god . . .

KLAY

Yeah, no; it's very real.

STEFAN

I guess I just don't get it.

NATE

What's there not to get?

ASHLEY	NATE
He's jelly—	I'm genuinely curious . . .

STEFAN

No I'm not; it tries too hard to be profound—

KLAY

You really have a problem with Terry, don't you?

STEFAN

Well—

KLAY

I'm sorry if you didn't want me to invite him—

STEFAN

No no—it's chill.

KLAY

Ok . . .

STEFAN

Listen. He's invited. . . . He's a decent guy—even if he doesn't have a filter—like I consider him a friend . . . we used to be quite close. . . .

IRIS

Who even let him into the scene? Was it you?

STEFAN

It was like half me, half Dave.

KLAY

What do you do Ashley?

ASHLEY

I'm a student.

KLAY

Where at?

ASHLEY

Tisch. For drama.

KLAY

Nice.

STEFAN

I ordered a pizza by the way.

NATE

Legit.

IRIS

No one is allowed to let me eat, ok? Promise. Don't look at me like that! I can't! It's bad! It's bad for my skin! Stop! No! Stop staring!

A buzz at the door.

STEFAN

I'll get it.

A knock. Terry enters.

KLAY

Yo Terry.

TERRY

Yo yo. What's up?

STEFAN
Just ordered pizza.

TERRY
I like pizza.

STEFAN
Everything I do is for you Terry. Everything.

TERRY
Words cannot express my gratitude.

KLAY
Who else is coming?

STEFAN
I think my cousin Olivia is stopping by. And Rosie. Maybe a few others.

IRIS
I'm embarrassed to be around people who are that cool.

STEFAN
Olivia's really not that cool, just vacant.

KLAY
I heard one of your songs at Clando tonight. Congrats.

NATE
Oh God, which one?

KLAY
I don't know the title; the one that used to be super popular; it had a lot of synths and was like minor key kinda, like—

NATE
It was probably "Radical Self Love".

STEFAN	ASHLEY
A real banger . . .	Nate, this is embarrassing, but—
IRIS	ASHLEY
	Uh—I was a pretty big fan when
Oh no what is happening?	I was in middle-school;
	like I came to a few of your shows.

NATE
Oh, no shit—

ASHLEY
Yeah, sorry.

NATE
No, it's cool. I appreciate it.

ASHLEY
No problem!

IRIS
He's nervous no one will like the new record.

ASHLEY
I really like it!

NATE
Alright . . .

TERRY
Big insecure creator energy in the room tonight.

KLAY
Are you still officially canceled Nate?

NATE	KLAY
Well, I don't have a record label. So.	
	It's gonna blow over.
I'm just releasing my own shit now.	
Like the old days.	You didn't do anything.

TERRY
I dunno, I think the Woke Inquisition is just getting started.

IRIS	TERRY
It's pretty crazy how people made up a bunch of rules for why you can't date coworkers, certain friends, teachers, people younger than you, or people older than you . . .	
	We're dealing with the ideology of a professional-managerial class that's increasingly, frighteningly powerful and basically theocratic.
conservative people, mean people, complicated people—	

IRIS

I think there's like this inhibition
against taking pleasure in power—

so

it comes out in all these fucked
up ways . . .

KLAY

I believe Nietzsche had something
to say about that—

TERRY

There's been a . . . total foreclosure
of moral possibility and imagination,
in our culture . . . a reduction of the
spirit of the laws to the letter of
the law . . .

NATE

Like. Imagine all your hard work,
your success, imagine all the shit
that gives you meaning—just being
like threatened for reasons that
are never clearly articulated . . . having
your finances attacked . . . your ability
to make a living attacked . . . losing
friends . . .

STEFAN

I'm sorry brother.

IRIS

Maybe we all need . . . to get a tiny bit cancelled, like as an inoculation.

KLAY

Probably.

NATE

I don't think you could handle ten seconds of what I went through.

IRIS

Probs not, true.

TERRY

We live in a very very sick culture. We should get rid of everything that's not been
means-tested by some kind of viable historical process. Like, now.

STEFAN

I think pessimistic, regressive traditionalism is a kind of tired position Terry.

TERRY

Sure, and I'm tired. So.

IRIS

You must be listening to all this and thinking *"what the fuck?"*

ASHLEY
    No, I'm just thinking in general.

KLAY
    I have to go to work in four hours. My entire nervous system is screaming.

STEFAN
    You have to get out of the cognitive proletariat.

KLAY
    This is why I need to write for your show motherfucker!

STEFAN
    I'm gonna try—

KLAY
    I'm just so over the editorial grind.

IRIS
    Can I smoke inside?

STEFAN
    Yeah I don't care.

TERRY
    Hi, I'm not sure we've met—

ASHLEY
    I'm Ashley.

TERRY
    Terry.

IRIS
    How did you and Stefan meet if I may ask?

ASHLEY
    He offered me coke at 169 Bar.

IRIS
    Aw.

ASHLEY
    I love your dress.

IRIS
    It's not designer, but I like to pretend it is.

KLAY
    I followed you on Twitter today Iris.

IRIS
That's nice.

KLAY
But you didn't follow me back.

IRIS
I'm withholding sorry.

KLAY
Fuck, I'm way too online aren't I?

IRIS
You're like, Tweeting as we speak, so.

KLAY
I am, it's true. Side-note: I tried to poop earlier, but there was no toilet paper.

STEFAN
Rolls are under the sink.

KLAY
Ah.

STEFAN
Also, who poops at parties?

KLAY
Me, motherfucker.

STEFAN
It's weird.

KLAY
Shut the fuck up.

TERRY
I've never in my life not pooped in my own home.

IRIS
Terry, Terry, Terry—

TERRY
Yes Iris—what's up?

IRIS
Oh so many things.

TERRY
Like what?

IRIS

 Should I become a nun? I've been fantasizing about convents lately.

TERRY

 Are you still doing a poetry MFA?

IRIS

 Yeah. One more year.

TERRY

 I'd like to read something sometime; I've heard good things.

IRIS

 I'll send you something.

TERRY

 Great.

IRIS

 I have been writing sooo much lately; I'm not sure if I'm inspired or emotionally out of control . . .

ASHLEY

 Is there a difference?

KLAY

 Are the podcast guys showing up?

STEFAN

 I don't think so, I think they're staying at Clando.

NATE

 I can't stand those guys. Why don't they just shut the fuck up about socialism?

TERRY

 Because that's all they have.

KLAY

 They want me to guest on one of their episodes.

STEFAN

 Good luck.

KLAY

 I went to college with Tim. He's a super nice guy.

TERRY

 Tim is extraordinarily stupid.

KLAY

 Oh well.

Another buzz.

STEFAN
I think my cousin's here.

KLAY
I always see her around.

STEFAN
She's ubiquitous.

Enter Olivia.

OLIVIA
Hello darlings.

ASHLEY
Olivia, I think I saw you outside Kiki's earlier.

OLIVIA
Oh yes. You must have.

KLAY
I always have to wait two hours to get a table there.

OLIVIA
You have to know the secret handshake.

KLAY
I think the secret handshake is being a lot cooler than I am.

OLIVIA
Honestly, yes. Sorry.

IRIS
You have iconic bone structure.

OLIVIA
I've been told before that I'm good looking in a way that is kind of banal and sexless, so
I don't think it's doing me much good. Is that Fernet Branca?

NATE
It is.

OLIVIA
Can I have some?

NATE
Of course.

OLIVIA

Is it completely obvious that I sobbed in Dimes Square tonight? I redid my makeup in the stairwell.

IRIS

You're perfect, don't worry.

OLIVIA

I've had an absolutely shit day—

STEFAN

What happened?

OLIVIA

Oh the photographer I work for was just in a vile mood and he kept yelling at anyone within earshot and I can tell he's at the phase of our working relationship where he believes that it is permissible to start touching my ass. Also, the model was clearly strung out from the night before and I was hungover and it was all so unpleasant. And then at dinner, I was with Caroline and James and they were fighting about something stupid—like something she said on Twitter that he found overly, and overtly, attention-seeking . . . and I was caught in the middle, of course . . . and they both kept appealing to me for moral support . . . which I am prone to give out of habit . . . Sorry to talk about myself immediately, everyone. It can't be helped.

ASHLEY

You're in fashion?

OLIVIA

So, I watched a documentary recently about young adults who were born into rich, influential or historically significant families and one of the subjects was a subversive Italian baron who said that the second question anyone ever asks you in America is *what do you do?*

ASHLEY

Oh gosh, I'm sorry . . .

OLIVIA

It's alright. It's just that . . . My career has been going downhill since I was about 9. . . . I'm at the *absolute* lowest rung of the ladder and it's quite appalling; my life is *quite* appalling . . .

STEFAN

Pizza's here.

He gets up and goes to the door.

OLIVIA
Sorry what's your name again? We've met before right?

KLAY
Klay. We met at Halloween last year.

STEFAN
Fun times.

OLIVIA
I mixed K and coke and threw up in your bathtub and cried.

STEFAN
I remember.

KLAY
Girl, you gotta be careful.

OLIVIA
I just do whatever anyone puts in front of me. If I die, I die.

TERRY
Is it cool if my friend stops by?

STEFAN
Everyone's always invited.

Stefan puts pizza down, but it mostly gets ignored in favor of coke.

KLAY
Is it Bora?

TERRY
Yeah.

KLAY
She's rad.

NATE
Who's that?

STEFAN
The DP for his movie.

OLIVIA
The one that's playing at Metrograph right now?

TERRY
Yes—and before that it was at BAMCinemafest—

IRIS
What's it called again Terry?

TERRY
'The Work of Fire'.

TERRY
Yeah, well.

OLIVIA
I was at the Q & A the other night—

TERRY
Hope you enjoyed it.

OLIVIA
I did.

NATE
It's good Terry.

TERRY
Thank you.

IRIS
How do you feel about all the attention?

TERRY
It's stupid.

STEFAN
Ashley is an actress.

TERRY
That's cool.

STEFAN
She's talented as fuck.

ASHLEY
He's saying that because we're fucking.

TERRY
I assumed, no offense.

ASHLEY
None taken.

IRIS
Do you model as well?

ASHLEY

    A little bit. Just like . . . —it doesn't matter—

IRIS

    You're so pretty; I would lick you except it's not socially acceptable. . . . Oh my god I'm making you uncomfortable; I'm so sorry.

ASHLEY

    It's all good.

IRIS

    By the way Terry, are you and Bora a thing?

TERRY

    No.

IRIS

    Why?

TERRY

    Because it's a friendship.

IRIS

    Ok but why?

TERRY

    Full disclosure Iris: I haven't had sex in two years.

OLIVIA	IRIS
Oof.	Why why why?

TERRY

    Because I'm trying to figure some stuff out and it's been good for my work.

STEFAN

    Has it?

TERRY

    It has, yes.

IRIS

    That just seems excessive.

TERRY

    To you—

OLIVIA

    Just get your dick sucked once and awhile. You'll be more chill.

TERRY

    I'm not trying to be chill.

IRIS

(picking up a slice)

    I need to lose ten pounds, don't I?

OLIVIA

    Stop it.

NATE

    Yeah, Iris—

IRIS

    Oh my god, you're all liars.

OLIVIA

    Iris, you're fabulous.

IRIS

    I've waited my whole life to hear that. I would say we should connect, but I already follow you on Instagram . . .

OLIVIA

    Oh you do? I should follow you back. I'm so bad at keeping track of that . . .

IRIS

    How embarrassing, but yes. I'd love that.

ASHLEY

    I'd love to connect as well; what's your—?

OLIVIA

    Here darling. . . . You all must come to my pop up next week.

STEFAN

    If I have to go to another pop up, it's going to be as an active shooter.

ASHLEY

    I'd love to stop by.

IRIS

    Same.

OLIVIA

    Lovely.

Terry picks up a book and looks through it.

TERRY

    There are over seven hundred questions in Augustine's 'Confession.' Not many of them get answered.

IRIS
You studied Classics?

TERRY
Classics and film yeah.

NATE   TERRY
Word.   Minor in French.

STEFAN
Do you wanna start a Delueze reading group with me?

TERRY
No.

STEFAN
Ok. What about a Benjamin reading group?

TERRY
No.

STEFAN
What about Adorno?

TERRY
Go fuck yourself.

STEFAN
Ok, what about Zizek—

TERRY
I'll kill you Stefan.

ASHLEY
Ya'll are intimidating.

KLAY
You're on your way to discovering that we're like the worst people in New York—

OLIVIA
No no—influencers—trust me on this one—are the worst. Then come art world people
. . . though they may not fully qualify as 'people'. After that are media people, which I
guess is this room.

ASHLEY
Nothing could be worse than hanging out in my dorm though; everyone just sits
around vaping and watching TV and not having a libido.

IRIS
Are they all getting fat?

ASHLEY
    Pretty fat, yeah.

IRIS
    That's bad.

ASHLEY
    I think I just expected people to be more interesting when I got to college, but they're simply not.

STEFAN
    The idea of post-suburban beta they/thems wasting their money on shitty marketing degrees while sitting around, watching streaming channels and eating vegan ice-cream from the tub fills me with incredible contempt.

OLIVIA
    Sure, but what can you do about it?

TERRY
    Choke on your own impotent rage.

NATE
    Sounds about right.

KLAY
    Stefan, question, have you even read half these books?

STEFAN
    I'm working on it; I've been on a book buying binge lately, so shit's just piling up.

OLIVIA
    Books are leisure class tchotchkes.

TERRY
    Well, they're also the basis of all intelligent culture.

OLIVIA
    I don't think that exists anymore.

IRIS
    No, probably not.

OLIVIA
    I sometimes forget that I have an Mphil in comparative literature.

IRIS
    That's hot.

NATE
    I never went to college. I don't regret it.

OLIVIA

I'm jealous.

NATE

I've been touring since I was 17, which is crazy to think about.

KLAY

Where are you from Nate?

NATE

Michigan. I'm actually supposed to go home and see my dad, but I've been avoiding it hardcore.

TERRY

Why's that?

NATE

He's not in good shape; he has emphysema—and I feel really guilty about seeing him. It's just depressing. Like, I bought him a house, but he has a lot of trouble taking care of himself at this point. He just sits around drinking beer and yelling at the TV. I dunno. My mom left him a long time ago and he's like a child at this point. He used to be into hunting, but he can't really move that well anymore. So. It's just completely fucked. I don't really wanna deal with it.

KLAY

Yeah, I'm also avoiding going back home to see my family. There are just so many disconnects; I'm not sure it's worth the effort.

NATE

I think the joke might be on me though because . . . on another level, home is really important to me in ways that New York or like LA aren't . . . and like, won't ever be. . . . It's just very easy to take for granted the things that you assume are always gonna love you back, or be there for you . . .

TERRY	OLIVIA
Right—	On the way over here . . .
I think that—	I was struck by the *intense* desire to go home—like outside of New York
um—	—home home—England I guess— and . . . as I processed that feeling . . .
nevermind.	I realized that I no longer had any real clue what that place was anymore. I've lost the thread.

IRIS

I grew up in Manhattan, so—

STEFAN

Should we go up on the roof?

KLAY

Is there any more coke? I kinda wanna do a line first.

NATE

I kinda wanna save some; we're going through it like water.

KLAY

What about Stefan's secret stash?

STEFAN

It's too early for the secret stash.

ASHLEY

If anyone wants some Adderall I have some.

KLAY

I'm very interested; I'm just not gonna sleep tonight . . .

ASHLEY

Cool, well, I'm happy to share.

KLAY

Rad, thanks.

NATE

Can we help carry anything?

STEFAN

I got the speaker . . . can somebody carry the beer?

NATE

I got you.

TERRY

I'm gonna stay here and wait for Bora. She's almost here.

STEFAN

Cool. You can find your way up.

Exit everyone but Terry.

He mills around.

Phone buzzes.

Apartment buzzes.

He answers.

After thirty seconds, Bora enters.

BORA

Where's everyone?

TERRY

Roof.

BORA

Should we go up?

TERRY

I just need to chill for a second.

BORA

What's wrong?

TERRY

I'm just not sure I'm enjoying myself.

BORA

Why?

TERRY

I'm socially paranoid; you know that. . . . I can't ignore my awareness that, if I wasn't here, they'd be talking shit about me—

BORA

Do you have any evidence of that?

TERRY

People go insane when you take yourself seriously—like your work, I mean. Most people are in a mediocrity pact with each other . . .

BORA

Anyone with real talent who acts with dignity toward that talent is going to trigger insecure people.

TERRY

I guess I know that, but it doesn't make me feel any better.

BORA

It should.

TERRY

I just had this idea . . . that people would adjust how they treated me after the film came out—like—as if I wouldn't have to adapt how I communicate and engage in all this trivial bullshit—

BORA

It's not your job to make people less trivial—

TERRY

 I think that's precisely my job, Bora.

BORA

 Your job is to make movies.

TERRY

 I would find it unforgivable in myself if I couldn't produce some kind of transcendence in others.

BORA

 You need to start going back to therapy, so I don't have to do the work.

TERRY

 I'm sorry; I'm pathetic.

BORA

 No—you're too gifted to be pathetic—

TERRY

 Aw, you think I'm special?

BORA

 Oh my god . . .

TERRY

 I kid, I kid . . .

BORA

 It just seems like you're having more success than you anticipated and now you're freaking out—

TERRY

 It's your success too—

BORA

 I think you want me to be as invested in your work as you are—

TERRY

 Do you even like it?

BORA

 The film? Yes. Of course. Relax.

TERRY

 But do you really?

BORA

 Yes.

TERRY

    Sorry. Like I said, I'm being paranoid.

BORA

    You are.

TERRY

    I'm just all over the place emotionally lately.

BORA

    I can see that.

TERRY

    I'm not over Julia, not even remotely.

BORA

    Have you tried reaching out?

TERRY

    She never answers.

BORA

    Ah.

TERRY

    Do you ever get obsessed with your exes?

BORA

    I don't get attached ever.

TERRY

    Oh.

BORA

    You need physical contact.

TERRY

    Probably. Can I have a hug?

BORA

    Uh. Yeah. You can.

They hug.

TERRY

    That was nice.

BORA

    Sure.

TERRY

    Anyway.

BORA

    I need a drink. I've had a long day.

TERRY

    What were you up to?

BORA

    I shot a commercial in Greenpoint.

TERRY

    For what?

BORA

    Like foot cream or something; I don't even remember.

TERRY

    Ah.

TERRY

    Stefan's been hitting me up about directing an episode of his new fucking show.

BORA

    Are you gonna do it?

TERRY

    I'm just not sure if it's a legitimate offer.

BORA

    Why wouldn't it be?

TERRY

    It's not clear, first of all, that it's his decision or that he has that degree of influence; and second of all, I don't think he would help me even if it was within his power to do so—

BORA

    Terry, then why would he even bother to bring it up in the first place? I don't get it.

TERRY

    Because that's how he gets people to gather around him: the vague possibility of career advancement—

BORA

    Or maybe he just thinks you're someone who would add value to his show.

TERRY

I think it's more complicated than that. Like, there's this cycle with him. First he meets you, and he's a bit standoffish; then, he flips, builds you back up, shows his charismatic side, acts like your best bud; then he starts to get cold again, distant, and the cycle starts all over again.

BORA

Where are you in the cycle?

TERRY

He's building me back up again.

BORA

Why do you think that is?

TERRY

I think he underestimated me and is sort of fascinated by the fact that I'm increasingly relevant and potentially even useful to him.

BORA

Say more.

TERRY

I dunno—why is Salieri obsessed with Mozart?

BORA

Oh my god Terry . . .

TERRY

I'm being ironic.

BORA

Are you?

TERRY

Maybe. Sure. Do you know he fucked Julia while she and I were still together?

BORA

I'm not surprised he tried, but I'm surprised by her.

TERRY

I think that the women in my life have always grown to resent me for my moral perfectionism and have used the first chance to escape to someone who demands less and is easier to like . . . fucking vibe with . . . I dunno. . . .

BORA

How did you find out exactly?

TERRY

She told me after we broke up.

BORA

And you've never said anything to him?

TERRY

I don't respect him enough to confront him.

BORA

Or you're too scared.

TERRY

No, no. I'm just gonna make a thinly veiled film about it one day, so that he knows what's up.

BORA

Terry, you're crazy.

TERRY

I like to be productive with my anxieties.

BORA

By refusing to talk to him about it directly, you're not giving him an opportunity to apologize and start over or move on. It's cruel.

TERRY

It's not my responsibility to make things easy for him.

BORA

I think you're afraid to lose his connections.

TERRY

No, I'm being strategic because I'm dealing with someone who is strategic.

BORA

You want to direct an episode of the show; I know you do.

TERRY

Fine Bora, you're right; I'm totally cucked.

BORA

I didn't say that.

TERRY

Do you know how fucking hard it was for me to make this movie? Do you know how fucking hard it will be for me to make the next one?

BORA

I do. Yes.

TERRY

There are so many things in my head that want to get out. That's all I care about. Scrounging for resources is a necessary evil. Dealing with sociopaths is a necessary evil.

BORA

Well then don't bitch about it.

TERRY

Fine . . .

BORA	TERRY
So—Terry—at this point, I need to be honest with you . . . I've had sex with Stefan too.	
	Wait, what the hell?
Yeah.	A few times . . .
I'm sorry.	Jesus Christ.

TERRY

When did this happen?

BORA

When we all met—in LA two years ago—

TERRY

Yeah and that's when he fucked Julia too. Freakin' unbelievable.

BORA

I had no idea.

TERRY

Look, I don't blame you Bora. . . . I mean, we're talking about someone who compulsively seduces people . . . charms them . . . as a survival strategy . . . basically unconsciously . . . and doesn't ever really even think about the consequences for others . . . and what's kind of sad is that I don't think of him as a bad guy at all—just someone who has dealt with his own sense of inadequacy in all the wrong ways and instinctually activates 'seek and destroy' whenever someone in the same generation demonstrates a greater degree of talent. It's like, it actually frightens me to know that I'm standing in his blindspot, because that's a very dangerous place to be and because I have a tragic streak already. . . . Like. . . . everything this guy does is calculated. He's privileged, precocious, smart—got to cut corners. He could drop out of college because he had connections in Hollywood. Could drop out of Hollywood because he has connections in the literary world. Now he can drop out of the literary world because he can sell his novel back to Hollywood. He's playing Call of Duty on easy—

BORA
Terry—question—how comes you never ask *me* about *me*?

TERRY
I don't?

BORA
No. You don't.

TERRY
You seem so self-sufficient Bora.

BORA
I have problems too.

TERRY
Like what? I'm listening—

BORA
Did you know my Dad is very sick? For instance?

TERRY
I did not.

BORA
Exactly.

TERRY
Is your dad gonna die?

BORA
Everybody's going to die.

TERRY
Why aren't you with him?

BORA
Because he lives very very far away and because he wants me to be doing what I'm doing.

TERRY
You're doing big things.

BORA
As I'm meant to do.

TERRY
See how can you be so calm and confident? It's amazing.

BORA

It's just like core, basic self-belief; it's nothing crazy. You're really tipsy Terry.

TERRY

I've been sippin' this thing.

A buzz.

Terry gets it.

It's Rosie.

ROSIE

Hey Terry, is everyone on the roof?

TERRY

Yeah.

ROSIE

Also—don't mean to be rude—I'm Rosie—

BORA

Hi Rosie. I'm Bora.

ROSIE

Nice to meet you. I'm gonna go up, but. See ya up there.

Exit Rosie.

BORA

Who is she exactly?

TERRY

Rosie. She's in the scene. I guess she's a visual artist. I could not care less.

BORA

Yes you do.

TERRY

People who attract a following without any discernible talent annoy me.

BORA

You resent everyone; I don't know how you function like that.

TERRY

Well, I don't function, so.

BORA

Right . . .

TERRY

On my first date with Julia, we just walked around Manhattan for an afternoon—and we ended up in the meadow in Central Park and . . . I remember . . . just lying there with my shirt off in the sun . . . and her head resting on my chest . . . all before we even had our first kiss . . . and just . . . looking at the clouds . . . just staring . . . happy . . . and I remember panicking because someone so beautiful was interested in *me*. . . .

BORA

Cool story Terry.

BORA

Right. I'm gonna go up—

TERRY

I'm putting on my shoes—hold on—

They exit.

Two

Enter Rosie and Klay, a little while later.

ROSIE
Where did he say the whiskey bottle was?

KLAY
One of the cabinets.

ROSIE
Cool. . . . I found it.

KLAY
Hey—

ROSIE
What?

KLAY
Rosie, you're so cute.

ROSIE
I'm ok.

KLAY
No, but I have a big crush.

ROSIE
Don't, I'm stupid.

KLAY
No, but really.

ROSIE
You should see through all my tricks; there's no reason to like me, I promise.

KLAY
What tricks are you referring to?

ROSIE
Asking you all those questions on the roof? Performing close listening. Inching closer. Batting my eyes. Letting you humble brag. Letting myself humble brag. Teasing you. It's just me on auto-pilot.

KLAY
Oh. I see. Can I still kiss you?

They kiss briefly.

ROSIE

    Klay—I don't think it's a good idea.

KLAY

    Why not?

ROSIE

    Don't you have a girlfriend?

KLAY

    Kinda?

ROSIE

    I heard you did.

KLAY

    So, I'm kind of dating this couple right now.

ROSIE

    How long has that been going on?

KLAY

    Couple months. I can see other people too obviously.

ROSIE

    Yeah man, that's great for you, but. Yeah . . .

KLAY

    Girl, I'm hear you. Vibes are off. My bad.

ROSIE

    It's just not my thing. I've been really into Catholicism lately, actually.

KLAY

    I gotchu, I gotchu. We're just here to get the whiskey right?

ROSIE

    Right.

KLAY

    I just want you to know that I've clocked the fact that you're different.

ROSIE

    What do you mean?

KLAY

    Than the others—

ROSIE

    How so?

KLAY
You just are.

ROSIE
Is that a good thing?

KLAY
Mostly.

ROSIE
I'm still not going home with you tonight.

KLAY
I know that, I think.

ROSIE
I like my men like I like my martinis—very cold, extra dirty—and you're only half of those things.

KLAY
I'm not even that dirty.

ROSIE
Exactly . . .

KLAY
I think I'm just feeling low confidence right now. Sorry to project that onto you.

ROSIE
It's fine.

KLAY
But hey, good news, I think I might get to write for Stefan's show . . .

ROSIE
Klay . . . you should stop talking about that . . .

KLAY
Why . . . ?

ROSIE
Well like . . . on the roof . . . when we were all talking . . . right after you walk away from the conversation, he goes '*what a fucking fool.*'

KLAY
That's really embarrassing.

ROSIE
I'm sorry.

KLAY
God damn.

ROSIE
I'm sorry! I shouldn't have said anything!

KLAY
Whatever, I don't care. Let's just go back up.

ROSIE
Can we do a bump first? I know where the secret stash is.

KLAY
Damn. Ok. Yes.

They proceed with the bump.

ROSIE
He's just feeling exposed, by the way, because his book actually came out and he's been talking about it for two years and it's ass.

KLAY
I guess. Thing is Rosie, I actually like his book. I admire Stefan. He works hard; he's hella smart. I just fucking wish he felt the same way about me; I wish he hadn't said that.

ROSIE
You're a good person Klay. Don't seek approval from people who are beneath you.

KLAY
I'm not particularly good; I'm just weak.

ROSIE
At least you're honest.

KLAY
I'm not even that. Not even close. The fact that you're even at the point where you're saying that is a sign that I've manipulated you a little bit. Being a good guy or whatever is my grift.

ROSIE
We've all got a thing.

KLAY
Yeah.

They exit.

Three

Bora and Stefan enter from the roof.

BORA

I really need to go.

STEFAN

Relax. Can we have a drink?

BORA

No no no no no—

STEFAN

Bora, she's asleep. She's a corpse. It's fine.

BORA

Are you sure—?

STEFAN

She's a lightweight. I know her . . .

BORA

I'm an idiot! I'm so stupid!

STEFAN

Chill.

BORA

It's wrong!

STEFAN

Oh my god, it's fine.

BORA

I feel like going in there and waking her up and apologizing.

STEFAN

No you don't; no you won't.

BORA

I actually want to.

STEFAN

So you can tell her how much you enjoyed getting your tight little pussy pounded on the roof—?

BORA

I hate that I gave into you . . .

STEFAN

Oh, you had a great time Bora, and you know it.

BORA

God, I don't need to get wrapped up in the whole sigma male con game!

STEFAN

I really dread these kinds of conversations.

BORA

What are these kinds of conversations?

STEFAN

Where you attempt to analyze me—

BORA

Can we at least talk outside? if we're gonna keep talking—I have to go anyway—

STEFAN

It's fine.

BORA

You wanna get caught—don't you?

STEFAN

She'd probably like catching us fucking, frankly. It'd turn her on. She's a little perve, that one.

BORA

I don't need to know that.

STEFAN

Suit yourself.

BORA

You surround yourself with people you secretly hold in contempt.

STEFAN

Maybe for lack of alternatives.

BORA

No, you actively cut out people who shine too brightly.

STEFAN

I think if you asked most people, Bora, they'd say I'm an extremely generous friend.

BORA

I've noticed you do this thing where you attribute your own views to other people, or the group. You'll be like: 'everyone thinks blah blah blah'—when the only person who thinks that is you. It's manipulative. You create perceptions that aren't there.

STEFAN

Where's this coming from? Are you talking about Terry's movie?

BORA

Which is also my movie—

STEFAN

Look, I think the camera work is great—fantastic.

BORA

Yeah, fuck off.

STEFAN

It is!

BORA

I feel bad for you.

STEFAN

Why's that?

BORA

Because the respect you crave has not arrived.

STEFAN

I'm doing fine thanks.

BORA	STEFAN
No—	
you have no respect for yourself . . .	I know my place in the world
. . . otherwise you wouldn't act this way!	and how to maintain it.
	It's normal
You don't believe in anything! And you hate anyone who does!	and it's healthy . . .

You hate them!

STEFAN

Did you fuck me just so that you could take a clean shot at my ego?

BORA

I don't give a shit about your ego; I'm just telling you the facts.

STEFAN

I'm not unaware of myself Bora. Truly.

BORA
> I'm skeptical.

STEFAN
> You know Terry's stuff is indulgent, like, objectively speaking. I don't know why you work with him. You could do better.

BORA
> Ahhhh Stefan—you're the Terminator. You don't even listen. You just keep going on. Terry and I work very well together. He's a totally different person during filming. He's someone who delivers, actually—which is why you envy him.

STEFAN
> Come on. "The Work of Fire." His shit's so pretentious.

BORA
> It's also insanely beautiful—

STEFAN
> Maybe at times—

BORA
> Admit it! It *tortures* you to hear me say that—

STEFAN
> Bora, I think you make all that beauty possible.

BORA
> No, it's a collaboration—

STEFAN
> Do you actually think he respects you?

BORA
> What? Of course he does.

STEFAN
> Haven't you noticed that everyone is just sort of a means to an end for him—?

BORA
> I know what you're doing.

STEFAN
> And what's that?

BORA
> It doesn't have a name, but you're doing it.

STEFAN
> He'll never treat you as an equal Bora—

BORA
 Will you?

STEFAN
 Funny.

BORA
 I'm so sick of you men and your pride. Why can't you all live in peace with each other . . . ? God, what am I even doing here? I've got to go!

STEFAN
 Hold up.

BORA
 Please let me leave.

STEFAN
 You don't have to whisper.

BORA
 I don't want to be here.

STEFAN
 Can I keep seeing you?

BORA
 I'm so disgusted right now.

STEFAN
 We have such an intense connection.

BORA
 What's wrong with you?

STEFAN
 What's wrong with you?

BORA
 A lot apparently! I really hate this!

STEFAN
 Let's go downstairs and have a cigarette, at least.

BORA
 I actually just need to sit here for a second; my heart's racing.

STEFAN
 Are you ok?

BORA

I just wanted to have a good time tonight. I don't know why everything has to be so complicated. I'm under so much stress. Holy shit. I cannot forgive myself for this behavior. It's so inappropriate.

Bora mumbles to herself in another language at length.

STEFAN

How about that cigarette now?

BORA

Is it absolutely necessary?

STEFAN

I can't let you leave like this. I'd feel weird.

BORA

Fine. One cigarette. Let's get it over with.

They exit.

Four

Late morning.

Ashley hanging out alone.

A buzz.

Ashley gets up to let in . . .

Rosie.

ROSIE

Hey, I left my notebook here. Do you see a moleskin anywhere?

ASHLEY

Ummm. Let me look. There's so much junk.

ROSIE

Stefan isn't here?

ASHLEY

Nope. He's at a meeting.

ROSIE

I see. Found my notebook.

ASHLEY

Do you want some coffee?

ROSIE

Actually, yes.

ASHLEY

What's in the notebook if I may ask?

ROSIE

It's not important.

ASHLEY

Ok . . . Do you even remember my name?

ROSIE

Ashley. I'm pretty sure we matched on Hinge a couple of months ago.

ASHLEY

Oh I did have my setting on "interested in everyone" for awhile.

ROSIE

Right right.

ASHLEY
I don't remember you, but I was really shy talking to girls.

ROSIE
Yeah I messaged you, but you didn't respond.

ASHLEY
Really?

ROSIE
Yeah, I'm pretty sure it was you.

ASHLEY
Are you like actually bi?

ROSIE
Sometimes.

ASHLEY
Yeah same.

ROSIE
Fucking a girl is kind of a way of deprogramming yourself to see them as competition.

ASHLEY
That's potentially true.

ROSIE
Do you have experience?

ASHLEY
Well I was trying to get some before Stefan.

ROSIE
So none.

ASHLEY
No ... well ... no.

ROSIE
Yeah. It's fun. Really.

ASHLEY
I know. I bet.

ROSIE
Are you and Stefan like, serious, or?

ASHLEY
I have no idea.

ROSIE
　　Ok . . .

ASHLEY
　　I like him, but.

ROSIE
　　But what?

ASHLEY
　　There's stuff going on.

ROSIE
　　Is it monogamous?

ASHLEY
　　It is not, currently. No. Can I ask you a question?

ROSIE
　　Sure.

ASHLEY
　　Should I like really invest time in his world?

ROSIE
　　Absolutely not.

ASHLEY
　　Why do you say that?

ROSIE
　　I think it's self-evident.

ASHLEY
　　You're all hot and cool.

ROSIE
　　It's a bunch of social climbers railing coke at 4am shitting on their so-called friends.

ASHLEY
　　That's bleak.

ROSIE
　　This whole group of people is not going to be hanging out in a year, let along six
　　months. It's rotting.

ASHLEY
　　You seem to be thriving on a personal level—

ROSIE

Yeah, because I'm one of those decomposer bacteria. What are your observations? I'm curious.

ASHLEY

A lot of people are out to be seen, obviously; talk to be heard; create to promote.

ROSIE

Right.

ASHLEY

The other night, we went out with his cousin Olivia, and her friends and there was this woman there, I forget her name, but she was just like holding court—like very charming, very cutting, very in command of the room—

ROSIE

Where were you?

ASHLEY

Lucien—

ROSIE

Of course—

ASHLEY

Yeah and like—she just seemed to know everybody and something about everybody and have all the connects with all these big name brands et cetera and there was just this moment where I was like, this person is cool, but like, they're just a chain of references . . . they're actually nothing—

ROSIE

Nope—

ASHLEY

They don't make anything, they don't feel anything, they don't make anyone feel good in any way. They can't give. They just neg the world and get rewarded.

ROSIE

Yup.

ASHLEY

I think I dislocated my jaw in my sleep . . .

ROSIE

So what's going on with Stefan's Netflix deal?

ASHLEY

Yeah, I dunno; it's happening.

ROSIE

    I mean, has he promised you anything?

ASHLEY

    Why do you ask?

ROSIE

    I'm just nosey.

ASHLEY

    He says he can probably get me an audition.

ROSIE

    Of course.

ASHLEY

    He's been vague. But.

ROSIE

    Get what you can while you can.

ASHLEY

    What do you mean?

ROSIE

    We have until we're about thirty—if we're lucky—before they replace us with newer models.

ASHLEY

    Is it wrong to wanna be on this show?

ROSIE

    If you can play the game, play to win.

ASHLEY

    Ok. I'm trying.

ROSIE

    Good . . .

ASHLEY

    Here . . . read this . . . it's the text Stefan sent me the morning after we met—

ROSIE

    "Ashley, here are a few things I want to experience with you: morning sunlight, Italian espresso, dreamy novels, linen sheets, a healthy dinner, hot bubble bath." Oh boy.

ASHLEY

    Right?

ROSIE

> Oof. Have you read his book?

ASHLEY

> A bit. And I read the pilot.

ROSIE

> I see.

ASHLEY

> It's fine.

ROSIE

> Yeah. I'm sure.

ASHLEY

> Does that Iris girl come from money, by the way?

ROSIE

> Why do you ask?

ASHLEY

> I just don't understand why anyone would want to spend time with her otherwise.

ROSIE

> That's a cunty thing to say.

ASHLEY

> I'm sorry.

ROSIE

> No, I like it. Also, she should NOT be dating Nate.

ASHLEY

> Yeah, seems complicated.

ROSIE

> It's a form of self-harm, actually. She might as well just take a razor to her wrists.

ASHLEY

> Do you want more coffee?

ROSIE

> I think I'm good. I'm already feeling too anxious.

ASHLEY

> Why?

ROSIE

> Life stuff. I like to convince myself I'm always on the verge of failure, starvation, and death . . . you know, as like motivation—

ASHLEY
>How's that working out?

ROSIE
>Um, not amazingly . . . because I do this thing where, instead of actually changing my worst habits, I just come up with new justifications for them. . . . Like, all my copes are like actively bad for my mental and physical health. Whoops.

ASHLEY
>That's your piece on the wall right?

ROSIE
>Yup. I don't like it.

ASHLEY
>I think it's nice.

ROSIE
>It's self-parody.

ASHLEY
>I wouldn't know.

ROSIE
>What's your biggest insecurity?

ASHLEY
>The sound of my voice. What's yours?

ROSIE
>I want bigger tits.

ASHLEY
>That's a good one.

ROSIE
>Tiny tits club right here.

ASHLEY
>Hell yeah.

ASHLEY
>How comes you haven't made a move on me?

ROSIE
>Paralysis of the will.

ASHLEY
>Oh.

ROSIE
   I'm all talk.

ASHLEY
   Damn.

ROSIE
   Yeaaaah.

ASHLEY
   Ah.

ROSIE
   Why don't you make a move on *me*?

ASHLEY
   I don't know how. I'm a baby.

ROSIE
   I think that's a front.

ASHLEY
   Could be. . . .

ROSIE
   You're like me: you know exactly what you're doing.

ASHLEY
   That's the attraction right?

ROSIE
   Or maybe that's the reason why the attraction can't go anywhere.

ASHLEY
   Damn.

ROSIE
   I'm not sure, if I'm being completely transparent, that I'm actually secure enough to embrace eroticism as fully as I pretend to.

ASHLEY
   Damn.

ROSIE
   Don't give up on me completely though please.

ASHLEY
   Maybe we can get a drink sometime soon.

ROSIE
   Sure. We can get a drink.

ASHLEY
> Cool cool.

ROSIE
> Yeah.

ASHLEY
> Can I tell you something?

ROSIE
> Sure . . . ? what about?

ASHLEY
> Something weird happened last night after you left.

ROSIE
> Ok . . . what's that?

ASHLEY
> Well you know how I passed out early?

ROSIE
> Uh oh—

ASHLEY
> Well yeah.

ROSIE
> What?

ASHLEY
> It's really strange . . . so Terry, Stefan's friend buzzed back in after he left.

ROSIE
> Ok . . .

ASHLEY
> And I let him and I was really groggy and he said 'do you know what's happening right now—?' And I said, 'no'—

ROSIE
> What was happening?

ASHLEY
> He said Stefan and Bora were fucking on the roof.

ROSIE
> Oh shit.

ASHLEY
> Yeah, but it gets a bit worse—Terry just like straight up kisses me—

ROSIE

Oh of course . . .

ASHLEY

Right?—and I'm very confused and just like 'what is going on?'—and I guess instinctively kiss back or whatever, but also kinda tried to push him away instinctively at the same time . . . and so I just kind of went with it . . . like I touched his cock and he was like so erect . . . and I was like . . . well . . . I was actually pretty turned on in a weird way by how turned on he was—like the effect I had on him—and then he asked me if we could have sex . . .

ROSIE

And how did you respond?

ASHLEY

Well, I just sort of sat there, stunned . . . and then he slumps to the bed and starts to fucking cry—like sob—

ROSIE

God, men are ridiculous.

ASHLEY

The whole thing felt invasive.

ROSIE

I'm sure.

ASHLEY

But it was also an enjoyable power-trip at the same time.

ROSIE

What happened with Stefan?

ASHLEY

Well, Terry basically ran away before they came back and I did what I always do . . . went back to sleep as if nothing ever happened . . .

ROSIE

Gotcha.

ASHLEY

I can't tell if I'm using Stefan because I'm scared of falling for him or if I'm falling for him because I'm ashamed I'm using him.

ROSIE

I can't tell either.

ASHLEY

I just don't know how much longer I can pretend to be this person who doesn't feel anything. I feel like I absorb so much pain from him and everyone around him and I can already tell that I'm gonna start to break down . . . if I don't take some kind of break . . . It's really overwhelming . . .

ROSIE

Are you absorbing pain from me?

ASHLEY

A lot.

ROSIE

Sorry about that.

ASHLEY

It's no one's fault.

ROSIE

No. Guess not. I'm gonna head out. Thanks. Nice talking.

ASHLEY

Let me know about that drink.

ROSIE

I will.

ASHLEY

Bye.

Rosie slips out the door.

Five

A week later.

Rosie, Klay, Olivia . . . also, two new guys, Dave and Chris.

Unclear what the situation is.

Mid-conversation.

CHRIS
I just want my fucking heart cut out or I want to be left alone.

ROSIE
Based.

CHRIS
I turned the manuscript down last year—so did Ian at FSG; I think I'm surprised it got such a big advance from Penguin—

DAVE
There's always a sucker.

OLIVIA
Truly.

KLAY
You're just jealous my guy.

Stefan's book is witty and erudite;
it's about beautiful, destructive young
people—and it's selling—so—whoever
bought that book made a great
business decision.

Your ego is out of control dude!

Out of fucking control . . .

DAVE

Fuck no.

First of all,

I got at least double for my last book.

Second of all,

the only modern writers I'm jealous
of are

DeLillo

and *maybe*

Pynchon.

ROSIE

Everybody needs to just simmer down . . .

DAVE

Klay, there was a time when I often had to choose between cigarettes and grilled cheese sandwiches, so yeah—I like being able to pay my rent and call up a primo coke dealer once in a while. . . . So do you guys want fairy dust lines or big fat ones? I could do either.

ROSIE

Fairy dust lines, please!

CHRIS

Have you read your cousin's book?

OLIVIA

I simply can't be bothered. Coming from a family of writers, it's simply best to maintain a strict 'I'm very sorry, but no' policy.

CHRIS

Makes sense. Love your mother's work by the way.

OLIVIA

Thank you. She helped Stefan acquire an agent, incidentally, so I consider that to be my contribution to his career.

KLAY

Dave, Stefan told me he asked you to blurb the novel and you said no.

DAVE

That is correct.

KLAY

So what are your actual thoughts? I wanna know—

DAVE

My thoughts would melt your face off.

KLAY

Come on.

DAVE

I don't want to speak ill of someone in their own house—

KLAY

Yes you do—

DAVE

Fine, but you might want to take shelter first.

KLAY

    I'm fine right here.

DAVE

    Whatever. I used to like getting loaded with Stefan because I thought he might be twisted enough to be original, but it turns out he just wanted to leverage the debut novel fetish for the sake of making people like him.

CHRIS

    In all fairness, he's still very young—

DAVE

    I don't care. It's an advertisement for what a good person his alter ego is.

OLIVIA	KLAY
Accurate.	Fuck that's so mean.

ROSIE

    I want more!

DAVE

    Klay, how you doing buddy? Do you need to take five? Go get your blanky and a lollypop?

KLAY

    Dude—

ROSIE

    Dave, I want more.

CHRIS

    She wants MORE Dave—

ROSIE

    More more more!

DAVE

    Cool. I'll just unload the clip.

CHRIS	ROSIE
Fuck yeah!	Yayyy!

KLAY

    Chill, people.

DAVE

    Shhh. Sentence by sentence . . . the novel is basically competent, but it's written from a place of extreme insecurity; it's like he's with you, the whole time, asking for constant reassurance and approval. He wants to turn every reader into the daddy who never loved him or the mommy he never fucked. Or the other way around: the daddy who never fucked him hard enough and the mommy who never loved him. Properly speaking, he should kill his father and fuck his mother, but he doesn't have the balls to do that either. . . . In fact, all he does, all he can do, is ask, over and over—to the point where you actually begin to feel morally and spiritually unwell—is ask: 'mommy and daddy, aren't you proud of me? I wrote a book about how nice I am! I'm a real man now!'

KLAY

Friends, I'm actually starting to feel very guilty.

DAVE

Why? Bloodsport is how you become a man.

OLIVIA

And—let's face it—Stefan almost certainly deserves it.

ROSIE

Savage. How long are you house sitting for by the way?

OLIVIA

I think he gets back on Tuesday.

ROSIE

Word. Also, that reminds me, you guys should come to my opening next week.

CHRIS

When is it?

ROSIE

Next week.

CHRIS

I'll be there.

ROSIE

But not just because I'm cute, but because I'm talented, ok?

CHRIS

Of course.

DAVE

I'll show up.

ROSIE

Amazing.

KLAY

Well now I guess I gotta. Where is it?

ROSIE
> Bushwick.

OLIVIA
> Oh, how quaint.

ROSIE
> Ouch, bitch. I came to your fucking pop-up.

OLIVIA
> Sweetness, I'm teasing. I'll try to make it.

ROSIE
> Mhmm.

KLAY
> I think I gotta call a car—

DAVE
> Don't be a pussy.

ROSIE
> Last night some annoying feminist scolded me for using the word pussy—

OLIVIA	KLAY
What a cunt.	I have to go home.

CHRIS
> Stop being a little bitch.

DAVE
> Yeah it's gay.

KLAY
> I'm being bullied.

ROSIE
> You love it Klay.

KLAY
> Do I?

DAVE
> Yes.

KLAY
> Maybe a little.

CHRIS
> Bullying is a form of mentoring.

KLAY

Mentoring is how older writers neutralize the threat of younger writers.

DAVE

Yeah, sure, so what's your point?

KLAY

I feel like you guys came up at a time when the scene was a lot easier to navigate—

CHRIS

Bullshit—

DAVE

New York was cooler, but I don't think it was easier.

KLAY

Can I please leave?

DAVE

No.

KLAY

I have an assignment due tomorrow; I shouldn't even be here. Fuck.

DAVE

Klay, I read some of your fiction.

OLIVIA	KLAY
Uh oh.	Yeah?

DAVE

Yeah, you've got a cool prose style man. Thanks for sending, albeit unsolicited.

KLAY

Uh, you're welcome?

DAVE

You just need an ending that's not so overwrought.

KLAY

Oh.

DAVE

I can give you some edits.

KLAY

What do you have in mind?

DAVE

Bro. Are you kidding me? You could be Norman Mailer; you could be James Baldwin; you could be Joan-fucking-Didion. Listen. I'm not gonna rewrite your ending for you. Tear up your ending and write your own new one from scratch—like a real fucking writer.

KLAY

I really cannot win.

OLIVIA

Those are the rules.

DAVE

I'm just trying to toughen you up.

KLAY

That's not entirely what it feels like.

DAVE

The first agent I ever showed my shit to not only stopped returning my calls, but apparently told other agents that I was a talentless hack. When I ended up getting the biggest agent, Binkie told me, 'I went with you specifically because those retards passed.'

KLAY

What are you doing Dave? Honestly—

DAVE

I'm hoping that you'll acquire a healthy ego through osmosis.

KLAY

By destroying mine? I don't get it.

DAVE

My friend, there's nothing to destroy.

KLAY

You're such a dick.

OLIVIA

I would love if someone destroyed my ego. I'm on the market actually Dave, how much do you charge?

DAVE

Bring me back some duty-free Gauloises next time you go to Paris—blonds—and introduce me to a few of those models you work with. They can be blonds, redheads, bald chicks . . .

OLIVIA

Deal.

DAVE

Is that Terry guy coming through? I like his shit—

ROSIE

You do? Interesting.

DAVE

He wants to adapt one of my books for his next film.

KLAY

Holy shit. Really?

DAVE

Yeah.

CHRIS

Who's Terry?

KLAY

Our auteur friend.

ROSIE

There's some weird stuff going on with him though.

DAVE

Yeah I've heard some things. He's got a lot of enemies in the scene, but, then again, so do I.

OLIVIA	DAVE
Were you referring to the move this Terry made on my cousin's girl; Stefan won't shut up about it—	Among other things—

ROSIE

Yeah. What do you think about her by the way?

OLIVIA

I think she's a real operator.

ROSIE

I'm getting a drink with her tomorrow.

OLIVA

Have fun.

ROSIE

I always have fun.

CHRIS

I feel like I'm breathing through my eyeballs right now.

ROSIE

Oh fuck.

KLAY

Chris, my dude, pace yourself.

CHRIS

I'm fine, this is just unbelievably good blow.

KLAY

You're not wrong.

ROSIE

Tonight is ridiculous in a good way.

DAVE

Yeah it was great running into you.

ROSIE

Aw. I love you Dave.

DAVE

Love you too Rosie.

ROSIE

I'm so tired of hanging out with people my age; the overall sense of cultural decline is deeply depressing.

CHRIS

My son told me this week that he's started taking estrogen.

KLAY

They're transitioning?

CHRIS

I don't even know what that means . . .

KLAY

How old are they?

CHRIS

Sixteen.

KLAY

Damn.

DAVE

The world is changing, man. If you wanted your kids to turn out like you, you shouldn't have had kids.

CHRIS

Yeah. Well. Sure. But I'm learning
a lot. More than I bargained for. But
it's good, it's good. I just want my
child to be happy.

ROSIE

Pass me a cigarette?

DAVE

This is the last one, just don't ash near the drugs.

KLAY

That's cool—

ROSIE

Oh damn—well you can have it—

DAVE

It's fine.

CHRIS

You know, I'm really starting to regret
farming my kids out to so many
nannies and tutors over the years.

ROSIE

What does your wife do?

CHRIS

My ex wife is in finance.

DAVE

I'm just gonna run down and buy more—

Dave leaves.

OLIVIA

So what's his deal exactly? Dave—I don't know him very well.

CHRIS

Dave is the proprietor of a decaying estate, like in a 19th century Russian novel, except his estate is the scene and we're the peasants who work the land.

KLAY

Some people think he wrote the best novel of the last ten years.

ROSIE

What's it called again? I think I've heard of it.

KLAY

'No Surprises.'

CHRIS

It's about a fireman who is scared so shitless on 9/11 that he refuses to get out of bed . . . and you know . . . respond to the call of duty. . . . But when he sees the second tower fall, he realizes the enormity of his cowardice and shoots himself in the head . . . But that's just the first third. The book is actually mainly about the fireman's widow who manages to do away with the corpse and defraud an insurance company . . . claiming, amidst all the confusion, that her husband died when the second tower fell. She gets married to a fireman who survived the towers—ironically I guess—has kids, and nobody ever finds out, including the new husband. It's really fucking good.

ROSIE

Maybe I'll read it.

OLIVIA

I read it in college.

ROSIE

Did you like it?

OLIVIA

I don't really remember much except for an entire chapter written from the perspective of the second tower.

KLAY

But the silent part about Dave that no one will say out loud is that he cannot bring himself to finish his next book.

CHRIS

Well, I do think he's worried that he's becoming more like the rest of us.

ROSIE

What's like the rest of us?

CHRIS

Incapable of truly astonishing.

KLAY

Oof.

OLIVIA

Nothing wrong with that.

ROSIE

I think the guy is just burnt out.

CHRIS

It's possible.

KLAY

Probable.

CHRIS

I mean, I think that's the risk that comes with committing both to an art form and to authentic decadence. He didn't do self-care and careerism; he lived.

OLIVIA

That's dramatic.

ROSIE

I think there's a tendency to mythologize people who squander their talent.

KLAY

Yup.

CHRIS

Sometimes, the act of squandering is part and parcel with the act of creating; you can't simply separate the two.

KLAY

I feel like you're carrying water for Dave just so that you don't feel like your own career was a waste; like you discovered him, cool—but like—let's have standards—

CHRIS

Dude, I know this whole scene is about third rate artists shitting on first rate artists, but . . . that's not my thing—

KLAY

Chill. Dave's just not that amazing.

CHRIS

You're clearly uncomfortable with the idea of an aesthetic hierarchy—

KLAY

I'm sorry, but I simply retain the right to not be that impressed. His shit's overrated.

CHRIS

May I ask if you've actually read one of his books?

KLAY

Uh—

CHRIS

Fuck, man—

KLAY

I've tried and it just repels me.

CHRIS

Why?

KLAY

His prose is unhinged.

CHRIS

Great literature deforms conventional language, forces a mutation; that's just how it works.

KLAY

He's jacking off into a tissue for six hundred pages a pop.

CHRIS

Certain writers, instinctively, sensing the threat from very stupid people, bury the sublime so far under the surface of irony that only very special readers can retrieve it—

KLAY

Uh huh—

CHRIS

And I'm guessing you're simply not one of those readers.

KLAY

Guess not.

CHRIS

Man, he's fucking *going for it* and that's awesome and you should care that he shares his coke with you and reads your shit.

KLAY

He treats me like a fucking subaltern. Fuck him.

CHRIS

Klay, you write fiction—or want to—right? So listen—he's not wrong to be hard on you and your friends; in fact, it's ethical. . . . People don't care about all the books that were almost as good as *Ulysses*; they don't read them, *they read* Ulysses. You don't read 'almost-genius'; you don't give a shit about 'well-made'; you don't tell your kids about meeting 'relatively clever' at a party. No. Hell no. You get hard for shit that will survive over time, that is the product of real existential blood and tears, or you don't get your dick sucked at all—you stay soft. Period.

KLAY

Chris—what are you talking about my man?

CHRIS

I'm talking about life amigo.

ROSIE
>Are you lonely Chris? You seem like it.

CHRIS
>Oh, certainly I am.

OLIVIA
>Say more—

CHRIS
>Loneliness is like a demon that crawls into your asshole and carves out a private hell—

OLIVIA
>Ok say less—

CHRIS
>You try to shit him out, but he clings to your bowels, howling. It's wild. Wild feeling.

ROSIE
>Yikes.

CHRIS
>To be clear though, I prefer my life now to where it was a year ago when I was still in my marriage. That was a significantly worse fate. Worse by a mile . . . I mean, you don't wanna get tangled up with serious personality disorder. . . . Like, I remember just going for walks in the middle of the night after my my kids would go to sleep because I couldn't stand being at home. I'd hit bars all over Manhattan and get really fucked up and talking to strangers and fuck strangers and cry and have a great ole' fucking time. A few times, I got knocked out because, after enough drinks, I'd start talking shit. But I always went to work the next day. Always. I've gone to lunch with major writers with a coke hangover and black-eye many times, and it's always gone great. I've acquired some major books like that.

Dave comes back with cigarettes.

DAVE
>Smokes.

ROSIE
>Divine. Thank you.

DAVE
>You're welcome.

ROSIE
>Thank you.

OLIVIA
>May I have one too?

DAVE

You may.

CHRIS

All these women I meet on dating apps stop talking to me like after two messages.

ROSIE

Do you realize how many messages women get on apps?

DAVE

I tried the apps for a month. The fact is, I spent two decades trying to keep boring people out of my life . . . and off the scene—but Bumble is a Miss America Pageant for boring people. Oh, you like tacos and you're addicted to NPR. Bitch, I've done more crack than Hunter Biden--

ROSIE

You've done crack?

DAVE

It was my response to the Iraq war. Anyway, the apps—not for me.

OLIVIA

They shouldn't be for anyone.

DAVE

I've always been more of a hunter in the wild.

A buzz.

Rosie gets up to get it.

KLAY

I went out with this model—who I was like bugging out about meeting—last night and like. She came back my house and we just held each other. No fucking. Super weird behavior for me. Like I'm legit surprised.

DAVE

Dare I say 'what a pussy'—?

KLAY

When was the last time you got any pussy Dave? 1995?

DAVE

I made love to my girlfriend at dusk today. It was quite passionate.

KLAY

I actually didn't need to know that, sorry I asked.

CHRIS

> We should go on a double date.

DAVE

> Last time we went on a double date Chris, your wife called me a narcissist and stormed out—

CHRIS

> Forgot about that . . .

Enter Iris.

ROSIE

> Your favorite people are here.

IRIS

> Oh my god, old writer-men! Yes.

CHRIS

> Uh—

DAVE

> Thanks Iris.

IRIS

> It's not ironic, I enjoy you. Also hello Olivia, lovely host.

OLIVIA

> Season's greetings.

IRIS

> Dave Dave Dave—

DAVE

> What's up?

IRIS

> I just wanna cry.

CHRIS

> Why?

IRIS

> Because tears are nice.

ROSIE

> Did something happen?

IRIS

> Yes, I'll tell you later.

KLAY
Guys, I'm actually calling a car.

DAVE
Shut the fuck up.

KLAY
This just isn't funny anymore. I'm leaving.

DAVE
Shut the fuck up and do a line.

KLAY
I will become a cautionary tale.

DAVE
You'll be fine.

KLAY
What am I even doing here . . . ?

DAVE
Coke.

KLAY
No, but I need to stop.

DAVE
You don't need sleep to go to work at a magazine on a Friday morning; trust me, I know from experience.

KLAY
I guess you're just built different Dave.

DAVE
I am, but that doesn't excuse you being a p-word.

KLAY
I genuinely and without exaggeration want to die right now.

CHRIS
Does anyone wanna drop acid this weekend?

IRIS
Last time I dropped acid I had an extremely long conversation with my vagina.

ROSIE
Same actually.

CHRIS
Cool. You can come talk to your pussies.

IRIS

I think I'll pass.

ROSIE

Chris, you're freaking me out.

OLIVIA

I've only tripped once and I do not need to experience it again.

CHRIS

What about you? I'm assuming you're a no Klay—

KLAY

I would love to do acid with your Chris, but I'm legit afraid you'll murder me.

DAVE

I'm not up for it either, sorry buddy. Every time I do acid, I just end up blowing lines of coke to make the acid go away.

CHRIS

That's fine. I'll have a great time by myself. Think I'm gonna drive to my place upstate. Feel free to change your minds. Just sayin'.

ROSIE

Thanks Chris.

KLAY

Ok. I officially called a car. Fuck everyone.

DAVE

I like your story dude, don't think I was criticizing you.

KLAY

Whatever. You were. It's alright.

DAVE

Just use more irony Klay. It's like salt in soup.

KLAY

Look, I don't know why I have to be the adult here, but just stop. Ok? We're not in high school—

DAVE

This is just a better, more narcotic version of high-school—

KLAY

That's horrifying. I'm leaving. Peace.

Klay leaves.

ROSIE

He tried to kiss me last week.

DAVE
Of course he did.

ROSIE
I started flirting with him so hard on the roof. And then I asked him if he wanted to come downstairs and have a drink with me. . . . I feel bad. Because. Yeah.

Klay returns.

KLAY
Forgot my keys. Whoops. See ya!

Klay leaves.

ROSIE
Anyway!

IRIS
Nate and I broke up tonight.

ROSIE
I suspected.

OLIVIA
It's for the best honestly.

DAVE
What happened?

IRIS
Many things happened. Can I read a poem?

CHRIS
If you like.

IRIS

(reading off her phone)

Impersonal people ran rampant like mice./ And I sat next to your voice at the piano./Threadbare all evening/ I was wondering if you had noticed me at all./ Meanings spawn upstream./ Fragments mark a rupture and a return./All this is put into question./Your bravura and aura, your/Blinded mouth kissing my teeth./One step further and they will banish us./So seal me away./I'm just sensitive enough to feel/What is happening now.

CHRIS
Cool.

DAVE

One step further and they will banish us, huh? So this poem's about you and Nate, right?

IRIS

Yeah.

DAVE

Apt.

OLIVIA

Iris, I have a friend who is doing a poetry night at this lovely and semi-secret club that I can't say the name of—do you want me to give her your name?

IRIS

Oh my God, yes. Please. That would be amazing.

OLIVIA

Fantastic.

IRIS

Also, I'm sorry about this everyone—but Nate wants to come over—he won't stop texting me.

DAVE

You told him you're here?

IRIS

He figured it out and it's only like two blocks from his place, so.

ROSIE

It's gonna be weird.

IRIS

I'll go hang out over there.

DAVE

Is that what you want?

IRIS

No! I don't know! I feel bad now!

ROSIE

Just stop answering your phone.

IRIS

No, that would make things worse.

CHRIS

Ask him if he wants to drop acid tomorrow.

IRIS
>Please no.

ROSIE
>Life is weird.

IRIS
>It's so weird! Holy shit! Should I keep texting him?

OLIVIA
>No, just let him figure it out that it's really over.

IRIS
>That's terrifying.

ROSIE
>Why?

IRIS
>I uh . . . the urge to text him . . . is just . . . it's just like . . . if I'm dating someone more broken than I am . . . like . . . fuck . . . then it's like . . . I'm not broken at all.

OLIVIA
>We've all been there.

DAVE	ROSIE
Well not me. . . .	For sure . . .

IRIS
>Yeaaaahhhhh.

CHRIS
>When I was in grad school, I used to have this recurring dream where I talked to someone named Mr. Yogurt and apparently, according to my ex-wife, I would yell "Mr. Yogurt has a master's degree in economics!" for some reason. Like I would be asleep, screaming "Mr. Yogurt has a master's degree in economics!". It was insane. I had to sleep on the couch for months.

ROSIE
>Sounds like it . . .

OLIVIA
>Hey—I actually think we should call it a night.

DAVE
>We're just getting started—

ROSIE
>Dave I adore you, but no we're not.

DAVE

Rosie, I always thought you liked seeing the sun come up?

ROSIE

It's up.

DAVE

Alright, then I'm taking these smokes with me.

ROSIE

Cool I'm actually trying to quit.

DAVE

I won't call you a pussy like Klay because I actually respect you, but—

OLIVIA

Goodnight Dave.

DAVE

I didn't even hear last call.

OLIVIA

Goodnight Dave.

DAVE

Olivia, I wanna get dinner with your mom next time she's in town—

OLIVIA

I'll get back to you on that.

DAVE

Alright

CHRIS

Iris, I can walk you home—

IRIS

I'm ok, but thanks Chris—

OLIVIA

Iris, you're welcome to stay here.

IRIS

That would be nice—

OLIVIA

If you want –

CHRIS

Ok. You wanna go to Odessa?

DAVE
    Odessa's closed.

CHRIS
    Really?

DAVE
    It's been closed for a couple years.

CHRIS
    I remember you me and Don used to go there to sober up after parties.

DAVE	CHRIS
Yeah, that was fifteen years ago and we had hair	
	Yeah we did.
and Don was alive.	
	Fuck.

ROSIE
    Olivia, can we help you clean up?

OLIVIA
    I'll clean shit up in the morning; it's fine.

DAVE
    We're coming to your show.

ROSIE
    Amazing.

Lights fade.

They slip out the door, making small talk.

Six

Late night at Stefan's.

Iris. Nate.

A few weekends later.

NATE

You realize the internal conflict this causes for me, right?

IRIS

Sure, I realize it. But I can't help how I feel.

NATE

Interactions like that are weird for everyone; it's complicated Iris.

IRIS

He wasn't just weird, he was rapey. He cornered her.

NATE

I think that's a *huge* stretch. Like. Stefan invited Terry to hang tonight only because he knew he could poison the room against him first. If it was that serious of a thing, he wouldn't put the two of them in the same room together.

IRIS	NATE
I dunno Nate.	Iris,
It just kind of bothers me that it doesn't faze you.	*He's* using *her* story to cripple a dangerous rival.
Like, I'm just realizing that I've been going along with the discrediting of the witnesses against you out of some weird kind of internalized misogyny and it's really not good for my soul.	Why are you with me then?

IRIS

I don't know; all of this is just occurring to me now.

NATE

I have trouble believing that.

Buzz.

Iris gets up.

NATE
Speak of the devil.

IRIS
Oh God.

Enter Terry.

TERRY
Yo.

NATE
How's life Terry?

TERRY
You know, could be better.

IRIS
Why's that?

TERRY
I, uh, just got off the phone with a buddy of mine from high school whose wife just gave birth, and the kid is pretty sick, like premature with a blood infection and my friend is just a mess over it. Needed someone to talk to, so I volunteered while I was walking over here. It's got me in a different headspace.

NATE
Which is what?

TERRY
I think . . . well . . . it really changes your perspective . . . like . . . as much as what's happening to Greg is terrible and frightening . . . I don't think he looks at his infant son in the ICU unit and thinks 'this isn't it'—just the opposite. He's filled with love. He's filled with purpose. But . . . when I look at my life, all I think is 'this is *not* it.' 'This *can't* be it . . . ' And I think that's probably true for most of us. . . .

NATE
Word.

Enter Stefan, Klay, Ashley, Rosie, Olivia.

STEFAN
They were out of Fernet, but I got whiskey.

OLIVIA
You're not pronouncing it right—

STEFAN
Fuck off.

NATE
That's fine.

STEFAN
What's up Terry?

TERRY
The opposite of down.

STEFAN
Right.

OLIVIA
I don't think I'm going to stick around for very long.

STEFAN
Why not?

OLIVIA
I have a shoot in the morning.

STEFAN
Alright, no worries.

OLIVIA
Are you going home for Christmas or?

STEFAN
I haven't decided yet.

OLIVIA
Let me know.

STEFAN
I will.

Klay goes to the bathroom.

OLIVIA
I did a Zoom with your mother and my mother the other day—

STEFAN
I don't like my mother.

OLIVIA
I know, but she is so proud of you.

STEFAN
> She's outrageous.

OLIVIA
> I love Lydia and I think you should see her more.

STEFAN
> Absolutely not.

IRIS
> Sometimes I see my face in the coke mirror, and I'm like is that really me?

ROSIE
> The thing about life is that it's absolutely terrifying.

OLIVIA
> Do you want a Xanax?

ROSIE
> I had an emotional breakdown less than 24 hours ago on the L train. So I'm still coping. And in the middle of my emotional breakdown my lover and I make a stop to pick up the girl we bring home sometimes for group sex. But she was really wonderful actually. In fact we all just laid on the floor and sobbed for a while before having a lot of really hot sex.

IRIS
> I wanna do that, but I don't want Nate to be there. And yes, Nate I am saying that out loud in front of you.

Klay returns.

KLAY
> Dude how do you NEVER have toilet paper?

STEFAN
> There's definitely some in the hallway closet.

KLAY
> Why didn't you tell me that? I thought you said under the sink—

STEFAN
> I switched things up just because I enjoy the bit so much.

KLAY
> Bro.

ROSIE
> Can I invite Dave and Chris to come by? They're at Clando.

STEFAN
Those guys kinda annoy me.

ROSIE
So I should tell them nothing's happening?

STEFAN
I dunno it's up to you.

IRIS
Why don't you like them?

STEFAN
I dunno dude, they suck. They're vampires. They've run out of careerist twenty-six year olds in publishing to fuck so they're expanding their hunting grounds—

ASHLEY
Who are we talking about exactly?

STEFAN
Oh these like literary world stock figures that we can't seem to get rid of—

ROSIE
I actually really like them both.

IRIS	TERRY
So do I.	Dave is a good writer, Stefan.

STEFAN
He's overrated.

KLAY
Yup.

TERRY
Ok I'm not gonna even say it—

KLAY
Say what?

TERRY
Well—you know—

STEFAN
What?

TERRY
Never mind. This is just a proxy war anyway.

STEFAN
For what?

TERRY
> You know 'for what'. Also, I'm going to win, just so you know.

STEFAN
> Ok.

TERRY
> That's it.

STEFAN
> Ok.

NATE
> Are we out of blow?

STEFAN
> We actually are for once. On second thought, Rosie just tell them to come, whatever.

KLAY
> I have some K, but I'm not sure we wanna go there tonight.

ROSIE
> Alright. You asked for it.

KLAY
> Are the podcast guys coming?

ROSIE
> I think later, yeah.

IRIS
> One of them keeps DM'ing to hang out; sorry Nate.

NATE
> I'm so far beyond caring.

IRIS
> Are you?

NATE
> I'm far beyond many things.

ASHLEY
> Can you pass me the whiskey bottle?

IRIS
> Yup—

ASHLEY
> Thanks.

IRIS

Can I read a poem?

NATE

Oh no—

STEFAN

Uh—

IRIS

Ok, that's no.

STEFAN

I'm sorry—

IRIS

No never mind.

NATE

Don't give me the evil eye.

STEFAN

NYU asked me to teach a screenwriting class there next semester.

ASHLEY

He won't let me take it.

ROSIE

Fucking the teacher was always my fantasy in undergrad.

ASHLEY

Same! I mean, it currently is.

ROSIE

Based.

IRIS

I just wish there was means of meaningfully dissenting.

KLAY

Dissenting to what?

IRIS

The way things are.

TERRY

Good luck.

ROSIE

There's something kind of fun about participating in a catastrophic civilization.

ASHLEY
　　Oh absolutely.

ROSIE
　　It's almost like going to church.

TERRY
　　Almost being the operative word.

IRIS
　　It's like, name one emotion that hasn't been frozen or neutralized by the uninterrupted harshness of monotonous stimulation—right?

STEFAN
　　Yeah, that's a tough one.

IRIS
　　I can't name a single one.

ROSIE
　　Blackpills for all . . .

KLAY
　　Random. Do you guys know Caroline?

OLIVIA	ROSIE
Unfortunately.	Oh my god—

KLAY
　　Yeah exactly—I went on a date with her last night.

ROSIE
　　How do you know her?

KLAY
　　Twitter.

STEFAN	IRIS
How was it?	You broke up with the couple??

KLAY	OLIVIA
Yeah I did. And, yeah, Caroline was a letdown. She was like hugely into sexting and like the build up, but in person she was just like completely devoid of interest. Also—total pillow princess.	I doubt she was particularly sober. . . . It's also probably the Botox as well . . .

A buzz, Stefan goes to get it.

IRIS
A poverty of subjectivity is *so* tragic.

ROSIE
I actually fucked her last winter.

KLAY
Oh shit.

ROSIE
She was definitely very different than how you described her.

KLAY
Different input different output I guess.

Dave and Chris enter.

DAVE
Sup bitches?

CHRIS
Yeah, sup—

STEFAN
The rumor is you have some blow.

DAVE
Remember when we used to be friends Stefan?

STEFAN
Vaguely.

DAVE
Yeah same.

Dan throws the bag on the table, Stefan takes it and starts drawing lines.

Iris and Nate do lines.

TERRY
I'm good with the whiskey, thanks.

STEFAN
What about you?

KLAY
Yeah, and I think I'm gonna do some K too on second thought if anyone wants some.

ROSIE
>I'm down. Thanks.

CHRIS
>What's the deal with ketamine, would I like it?

KLAY
>Chris, I legit think you'd love it.

CHRIS
>Ok, I'll give it the old college try.

ASHLEY
>I have class in the morning.

STEFAN
>You're fine.

ASHLEY
>Ah, I shouldn't. . . .

STEFAN
>You're really fine.

KLAY
>You're the devil.

STEFAN
>Something like that . . .

CHRIS
>When I was in grad-school, I used to have this re-occurring dream about this man named Mr. Yogurt—

DAVE
>Chris—

CHRIS
>What?

OLIVIA
>We've heard that one before.

ASHLEY
>Who is Mr. Yogurt?

ROSIE
>We're all Mr. Yogurt.

ASHLEY
>Oh, ok. Makes sense.

NATE

We're living through the dumbest time in human history.

TERRY

Let's try not think about it.

OLIVIA

Yeah. Let's not . . .

The coke gets passed around.

A buzz.

DAVE

The podcast guys just texted me. They're downstairs.

Blackout.

Minotaur

"Combien de choses nous servoyent hier d'articles de foy, qui nous sont fables aujourd'huy?"

—Montaigne

This version of *Minotaur* premiered at Forgotten Works Studio in Dumbo, Brooklyn in June of 2022 with the following cast:

Clara*: Cassidy Grady
Maud*: Eliza Vann
Theo: George Olesky
Doug: Bob Laine
Edith: Meg MacCary
*Katie Kane and Mary Nealy were alternates as Clara and Maud, respectively.

Directed by Michael Segal
Set Design by the cast
Lighting Design by Duncan Davies
Stage Managed by Aubrey Mann

Produced by Gabrielle Bluestone and Matthew Gasda

Cast of Characters

Clara: 27, writer
Maud: 30, in finance
Edith: 55, a lawyer, married to Doug, step-mother to the girls
Theo: 30, Edith's son, filmmaker, bartender
Doug: 60, an architect

Setting:

A highly modern house in the country.
The stage is split up between two discrete spaces: a bathroom, a kitchen.
The scenes alternate between these two locales.

One

A bathroom, with a bathtub.

Clara takes a bubble-bath and drinks a glass of wine. Her sister Maud sits against the door. Maud is also drinking wine.

Maud gets up, opens the window, and puts her wine-glass on the windowsill. Maud takes a cigarette from her shirt pocket.

CLARA
Edith is gonna kill us.

MAUD
She's not going to find out—

CLARA
Can you hand me my phone?

MAUD
Why are we not at the hospital with Pop-pop?

CLARA
Because.

MAUD
I wish he and Dad would just like, forgive each other.

CLARA
It's not gonna happen at this point.

MAUD
Why not?

CLARA
Because it just won't. Here, take my phone back, I don't want it to get sudsy.

MAUD
You live on that thing.

CLARA
Are you gonna tell Edith and Dad about the engagement?

MAUD
Eventually.

CLARA

It's awkward right?—having to convince people of something you've not convinced yourself of—

MAUD

Just because your love-life is a mess . . .

CLARA

If you're implying that I'm jealous: no I'm not, fuck no—

MAUD

You're trying to make me feel as shitty about myself as I feel about yourself—

CLARA

Ideally. Can you hand me my phone again?

MAUD

No.

CLARA

Why not?

MAUD

You need to disconnect.

CLARA

Gimme the phone dude.

MAUD

One bathtub selfie is enough.

CLARA

Not for my followers.

MAUD

It's gross the way you scrape together a meaningful image from meaningless experiences. Like, just because you went to Vassar and became a situational lesbian doesn't mean—

CLARA

I'm sorry, what?

MAUD

I mean, like, haunting literary parties, getting a book deal to write about yourself—

CLARA

First of all, you're one to talk—especially about situational lesbianism—

MAUD

Excuse me?

CLARA
>In high school? Those so-called sleepovers—

MAUD
>That doesn't count!

CLARA
>And second of all, you don't even read my writing—

MAUD
>Because I like to keep my food down—

CLARA
>You didn't use to.

MAUD
>Another cheap shot!

CLARA
>Dad told me he wants to get an apartment in the city, just for himself.

MAUD
>That's kind of a bad sign for his marriage—

CLARA
>Who cares?

MAUD
>They seem happy though.

CLARA
>'Seem.'

MAUD
>You refuse to see the good in people—

CLARA
>You refuse to see anything *other* than the good in people—

MAUD
>It makes me really sad to talk to you sometimes.

CLARA
>Just be glad that you're not me and move on.

MAUD
>I admire you—

CLARA
>Mistakenly—

MAUD

But I can't keep up with you sometimes . . .

CLARA

Don't court my approval, please.

MAUD

I wanna to be friends.

CLARA

Friendship is so banal.

MAUD

We used to be so close . . .

CLARA

When we were children—

MAUD

There's a bond—

CLARA

No, there's guilt over the lack of a bond.

MAUD

Guilt is a kind of bond.

CLARA

Guilt is a very profound form of torture. I got a text—

MAUD

Someone named Sarah Nicole—

CLARA

My editor—give it here—please don't read it.

MAUD

I'm not, chill.

MAUD

You're in love with her—

CLARA

Vaguely.

MAUD

Honestly, can you just tell me once and for all if you're really a dyke?

CLARA

No.

MAUD

'No' as in 'you're not' or no as in 'you won't tell me?'

CLARA

'No' as in 'go fuck yourself.'

MAUD

Thanks.

CLARA

You're afraid of anything that violates the little moral paradigm you've built with super-glue, tape, and Catholic guilt; I guess you think it keeps you safe—

MAUD

I've not, for a single second of my life, felt safe.

CLARA

So let's talk about that: your 'not feeling safe'—

MAUD

Hell no.

CLARA

Why not?

MAUD

Because I'm not really talking to my sister, I'm talking to 'Clara' the gossip columnist, the internet personality, the erotic self-help writer—

CLARA

Clara the third-rate hack is as much a performance as Maud the first-rate hausfrau—

MAUD

I can't deal with people who sound so sure of themselves when I don't feel sure of anything.

CLARA

Sounding sure is not being sure—

MAUD

I know.

CLARA

Because neither of us are sure about anything. Can you just give me my phone?

Maud takes the phone and tosses into the tub, where it lands with a plop. Clara frantically tries to save it.

CLARA

I could have been electrocuted.

MAUD

I doubt it.

CLARA

Now I have no connection to the outside world. When I go literally insane, you have only yourself to blame.

MAUD

How will I live with myself?

CLARA

The same way you always do: with the overwhelming force of self-deception.

MAUD

That's not fair.

CLARA

Of course it is. For instance: explain to me why you're getting married to a closeted investment banker—

MAUD

Look—

CLARA

I know, I know: you love each other—

MAUD

But we do!

CLARA

You mean: you like the same interior decorating catalogues.

MAUD

Stop making assumptions.

CLARA

Is it that you feel more attractive when he makes you dress up as a boy?

MAUD

Oh my god, *stop*—

CLARA

I'm having too much fun.

MAUD

Pop-pop asked me this morning why we don't visit him more often.

CLARA

I don't like doing things just for the sake of doing them.

MAUD

He's dying—

CLARA

Everyone's dying.

MAUD

He's scared. He's alone.

CLARA

Everyone's scared. Everyone's alone.

MAUD

You know what I mean.

CLARA

Death-bed selfies do not fit my Instagram aesthetic.

MAUD

In a few days, he's gonna be gone forever.

CLARA

And in the scheme of eternity, it will not matter if I visited him for two hours before he died.

MAUD

But in the scheme of his life, it will.

CLARA

Hey, we should put my phone in a bowl of rice.

MAUD

Fuck your phone.

CLARA

Can you please leave?

MAUD

I'm trying to avoid cocktail hour.

CLARA

Cocktail hour is the *worst* . . .

MAUD

You don't realize how much I have to apologize to other people for your behavior—

CLARA

That's just your own sense of shame and propriety kicking in.

MAUD

You get off when you write something controversial and the internet blows up—

CLARA

Just leave the bathroom Maud—

MAUD

I can't.

CLARA

Why not?

MAUD

Because you won't admit that you're vulnerable; you won't *be* vulnerable.

CLARA

So what?

MAUD

I'm tired of this loafer posture.

CLARA

So am I.

MAUD

Just say that life hurts you too.

CLARA

You want to have the power to make me feel like shit.

MAUD

Because you make me feel like shit—

CLARA

No, I just point out the ways in which you intentionally prevent yourself from taking any real risks in life—

MAUD

I don't intentionally do anything—

CLARA

Which is precisely your problem.

MAUD

But not yours . . .

CLARA

Oh no: I'm very intentional. For instance, I feel like the best life hack for me is only dating, like, 40-year-old male creatives obsessed with their careers.

MAUD

But that sounds horrible.

CLARA

Half a woman's life is wasted splurging to help and console others. But men don't do that, which is admirable. So I want to be more like them, rather than less.

MAUD

Empty and self-satisfied?

CLARA

Sure.

MAUD

Sometimes I can't listen to you talk. It's just verbal Instagram—like why even use words?

A knock on the door.

CLARA

What the fuck . . . ? *Who is it?*

EDITH

I brought you some rice.

CLARA

Were you listening to our conversation?

EDITH

I just heard the phone thing. I'm sorry. But do you want the rice or not?

CLARA

Bring forth the sacred rice.

EDITH

Is that a yes?

CLARA

YES.

Enter Edith, with cooked rice.

CLARA

Did you cook this?

EDITH

I microwaved it; I thought—

CLARA

Edith, it needs to be dry rice to absorb the water. Jesus Christ.

EDITH

I'm sorry . . .

CLARA

It's fine. Just take my phone, and put it in some dry rice downstairs.

EDITH

Alright . . .

CLARA

Thank you Edith. Don't pout.

EDITH

You're welcome . . .

Exit Edith.

CLARA

I'm thinking about Mom.

MAUD

Oh.

CLARA

She was the last person to die in the family. I just realized. My feet are getting cold.

MAUD

Get out then—

CLARA

No, I'm comfortable.

MAUD

Mom used to take long baths too.

CLARA

This bath is an homage.

MAUD

Clara . . .

CLARA

I can't believe you don't think I show vulnerability.

MAUD

Missing Mom isn't being vulnerable.

CLARA

Yes it is.

MAUD

No, missing Mom is missing Mom. Being vulnerable is something else.

CLARA

Sure.

MAUD

Do you really think Marco's gay?

CLARA

Don't you?

MAUD

It's not that simple.

CLARA

I know.

MAUD

You want to start unraveling little bits of me without really wanting to do justice to the whole picture—

CLARA

You go to the dog park in the mornings, after coffee, then you come back and have eggs and a little endive salad. Always endive. It's so decadent. And then Marco wakes up and you talk and he gets ready for work and you get ready for work and he jacks off to the sight of construction workers jackhammering outside. There, that's the whole picture.

MAUD

We wanna have kids.

CLARA

Matrimony is like setting up a limited liability corporation for the enterprise of procreation.

MAUD

I want little children who scamper across hardwood floors in bare feet; I want a dog who barks at the mailman. I want to go to parent-teacher conferences and hear how gifted my children are.

CLARA

I don't.

MAUD

But I wonder if I'm trying to compensate for our childhood being essentially a failure . . .

CLARA

It think it's a safe bet that that's exactly what you're doing.

MAUD

It's really frustrating that you just want to cut yourself off from our past—

CLARA

All we do in this family is talk about Mom.

MAUD

That's not what I'm saying—

CLARA

Whatever.

MAUD

I don't want to go to mass.

CLARA

Then don't go.

MAUD

But we have to—

CLARA

No we don't; I'm not.

MAUD

If Dad wants to—

CLARA

We can do whatever we want.

MAUD

No we can't.

CLARA

I guess we'll find out. What time is Theo getting here?

MAUD

No idea . . .

CLARA

You think Dad would be happier if he relied more on *you* than Edith—don't you?

MAUD

You refuse to acknowledge that you have the same problems you point out in other people—

CLARA

I acknowledge my weaknesses all the time . . . constantly in fact—

MAUD

But you don't *feel* to other people like you do.

CLARA

That's not my problem. I wonder if my phone's ok—

MAUD

Relax.

CLARA

You're making me anxious—

MAUD

It's funny, I don't believe in life after death, but I believe in a life after death for Mom . . .

CLARA

Mom is ash and nothingness. Give me my towel—

MAUD

Church is going to be so gloomy tonight.

CLARA

My feet are cold: gimme me the towel.

MAUD

You don't have to be such a bitch.

CLARA

You can't let so much of the world in Maud: it's too exhausting. Just gimme the goddamn towel.

Maud hands Clara the towel.

MAUD

It hurts me that you don't admire me the way I admire you . . .

CLARA

Get over it.

Exit Clara.

Exit Maud.

Two

Edith and Clara in the kitchen, mid-conversation, wine in hand.

CLARA

I've been drinking since this afternoon.

EDITH

Pretty typical for you.

CLARA

I'm starting to feel guilty about skipping mass.

EDITH

I guess it's nice to know you have a moral conscience.

CLARA

It really shook me that *Theo* went. *Theo*—

EDITH

He likes to confound expectations.

CLARA

Was he always like that?

EDITH

I believe so, yes.

CLARA

There's something comforting about the idea that people have intrinsic natures; I really prefer it to the idea that we can choose who we are . . . that's too much responsibility.

EDITH

Oh, I don't think people choose much at all, don't worry.

CLARA

Are there any more of those cookies left?

EDITH

Yes, would you like some?

CLARA

My sugar tooth is thwobbing.

EDITH

I'll get you a plate.

Edith fetches the cookies.

CLARA
>Do you want some?

EDITH
>No thank you; I'm watching what I eat these days.

CLARA
>I'm not: tryna die by thirty over here.

EDITH
>Clara, this *persona* of yours really grates on me.

CLARA
>'Persona' sounds so superficial. I prefer 'highly ornate, well-wrought public performance.'

EDITH
>Ok: your 'highly ornate, well-wrought public performance' is rapidly wearing thin.

CLARA
>Thank you, that's better.

EDITH
>You're a very emotional person Clara, but I think you're afraid to show it.

CLARA
>Blah blah blah.

EDITH
>Why don't you ever express it? Let out some of those feelings?

CLARA
>In front of *you*? Uh. No, Edith. No thanks.

EDITH
>You always like to turn me into the bad guy.

CLARA
>If the shoe fits.

EDITH
>Sometimes I think that I'm the only person in this family with an actual empathy for others—

CLARA
>Oh that's a joke.

EDITH
>Is it?

CLARA

    Oh certainly, certainly.

EDITH

    Why?

CLARA

    People are your means to your ends.

EDITH

    Thanks for that.

CLARA

    I'm serious: I *see* you Edith—

EDITH

    Great.

CLARA

    You're the grand chess master my friend.

EDITH

    What exactly is your evidence? What have I done? When have you actually observed—

CLARA

    In mine mind's eye.

EDITH

    That wouldn't stand up in court.

CLARA

    This isn't court; this is kitchen.

EDITH

    But you see my point—

CLARA

    Do you see mine? This is a domain—one on one, with me—where you can't use technical tricks to win. You can't adjust what's within me, can't adjust how I see you. . . .

EDITH

    Alright Clara.

CLARA

    You didn't want daughters. You had no use for us. We were the free shit that got thrown into the pre-nup. You would've sold us at a yard sale if you could've gotten away with it.

EDITH

    Second marriages are complicated.

CLARA

Yeah. And to this day, I still do not understand precisely what you got out of the whole arrangement.

EDITH

I was a young, single mother: it's that simple.

CLARA

So what? Be strong bitch.

EDITH

Excuse me? Easier said than done. I mean—*you try it Clara*—

CLARA

Mm, no thanks.

EDITH

I always sort of blamed you for holding Theo back—

CLARA

What the fuck does that mean?

EDITH

Well . . .

CLARA

He hates you more than I do. You should talk to him about it.

EDITH

I don't think my son hates me; I think you're conveniently projecting your own feelings onto others. Perhaps that makes you feel more secure.

CLARA

You're such a smug-ass cunt.

EDITH

Even as a teenager, when you first met, you needed Theo to be on your side, just like you needed to dominate your relationship with your sister and your father. You attack me because I'm the only person who questions your special status, your exempt status. You don't wanna play by a special set of rules your whole life Clara—that's not the point of intelligence . . .

CLARA

What's the point then?

EDITH

Let me finish—

CLARA

I'm waiting— . . .

EDITH

I think . . . the more clearly you see the things, the less of an excuse you have for acting like everybody else . . . of using emotions to bludgeon . . . as power . . .

CLARA

You think I do that?

EDITH

You switch on your moods on . . . like music . . . whenever you want to manipulate the way other people are behaving; you have an intuitive awareness of how authoritative those moods are . . . and you have no compunction about keeping other people in a state of constant fear that you might attack . . .

CLARA

Do you really think that's true? Do you really think that's fair?

EDITH

Who knows. I guess it's just something I want you to think about. So think about it.

CLARA

Never.

EDITH

It's ok: I can see that what I said has . . .

CLARA

I feel like I'm back in the same vulnerable place I was before, at sixteen, being here . . . I *really* don't like it . . .

EDITH

Ok Clara. I'm gonna go lie down; I have a headache.

CLARA

Mhm. Bye.

Exit Edith.

Gradual blackout.

Three

The bathroom.

Enter Maud and Theo, hot and heavy.

MAUD
  We're gonna wake the whole house up.

THEO
  Who cares?

MAUD
  I wish we could *just* talk for once.

THEO
  No you don't.

MAUD
  I scare myself when I'm with you.

THEO
  I'm not sure what you mean by that.

MAUD
  There are layers.

THEO
  To what?

MAUD
  To me.

THEO
  All I could think about on the drive up was the taste of your skin.

MAUD
  Go away.

THEO
  I'm a part of your life.

MAUD
  I feel like I've been flayed.

THEO
  You talk about being turned on like it's a religious experience.

MAUD

    I mean . . .

THEO

    That's not my style.

MAUD

    You were so graceful when you were absent from my life. But now that you're here, you just seem contorted and ugly.

THEO

    Cool.

MAUD

    Did I hurt you right there?

THEO

    No.

MAUD

    I can't seem to sufficiently hurt people. I wonder what I'm doing wrong.

THEO

    Everything you say is an attempt to hurt yourself, that's why.

MAUD

    It's pitiful.

THEO

    A little bit.

MAUD

    Why did you stop responding to my texts?

THEO

    You told me not to respond even if you tried to contact me. Remember?

MAUD

    I didn't know what I wanted . . .

THEO

    No, you didn't like what you wanted.

MAUD

    I snuck into your room every night for two years. When you went to college, I would lay in your bed and masturbate. No joke. I would push my nose into your pillow, bury my head in your clothes. . . .

THEO

    Your voice is like the feeling of the wind before it starts . . .

MAUD

You're just a major episode in the rejection I have been undergoing my entire life: from my father all the way up to now.

THEO

You rejected me—

MAUD

Shut up fuckface. Self-preservation.

THEO

Alright.

MAUD

Dread dread dread—

THEO

Of what?

MAUD

Tomorrow, everything—

THEO

I can hear your blood-murmur—

MAUD

You're so close—

THEO

Fuck: I miss my younger self.

MAUD

Why? Because you never attained status higher than hot bartender? That's a pretty good status. I know some people would kill for that status.

THEO

Like your boyfriend?

MAUD

Fiance—

THEO

Shit.

MAUD

Are you jealous of him?

THEO

No.

MAUD

Why do we have better sex than we have with other people?

THEO

Because we've found a way to both be selfish at the same time.

MAUD

I can't decide whether you're a piece of shit, or whether I wish was getting married to you instead of someone else.

THEO

Why am I potentially a piece of shit?

MAUD

You went to college and had fucked other girls while I was stuck here, falling apart.

THEO

So what?

MAUD

Did it ever occur to you that if my mother hadn't died, I would have never met you?

THEO

That has occurred to me, yes.

MAUD

I can't forgive myself for being *ok* with that trade-off.

THEO

I'm not convinced you care about any of the things you say you care about.

MAUD

You're such a jerk.

THEO

It was really weird for me when I figured out that sexual love was the thing that was keeping your dad and my mom together.

MAUD

You think that's what it is?

THEO

I mean, sex is what's keeping this whole family together.

MAUD

It's weird.

THEO

You like starting puzzles but not completing them.

MAUD
>You're not a puzzle.

THEO
>Why, because I don't hide the fact that I like—

MAUD
>Because you don't change over time—

THEO
>I don't?

MAUD
>No. You were a bonerface when I met you and you're a bonerface now.

THEO
>Uhuh.

MAUD
>You're one of those guys who think he's deep because classical music makes you cry, the kind of guy who rewatches his old student films and secretly thinks he was a misunderstood genius—

THEO
>Keep going.

MAUD
>No, I feel satisfied.

THEO
>And you didn't even need to get undressed—

MAUD
>Don't act so hurt.

>*Maud opens the window.*

THEO
>It's fucking freezing—

>*Maud lights a cigarette and leans her head out the window.*

MAUD
>The stars are out.

>*Theo walks up to Maud, takes the cigarette from her hands, throws it in the bathtub, and kisses her.*

They break apart.

MAUD
Now I have to light another one.

THEO
I feel like I'm always waiting for you to make up your mind about me.

MAUD
I made up my mind when I was sixteen.

THEO
And what did you decide?

MAUD
That you were insurance against the condition of being alone.

THEO
Pass me that cigarette.

MAUD
Honestly, I still just feel like all you want to do is fuck.

THEO
That's not true—

MAUD
Then what *do you* want Theo?

THEO
The emotional stakes lowered enough so that I can jump over them.

MAUD
Coward.

THEO
Obviously.

MAUD
You don't have to be real, you just have to fool me.

THEO
We've been having the same conversation for ten years.

MAUD
How do we get out of the loop?

THEO
We could just switch roles: you play the sexual manipulator and I play the victim.

MAUD

Ok great let's do it; I'd find that more interesting.

THEO

You were so graceful when you were absent from my life, but, now that you're here, you just seem contorted and ugly.

MAUD

Cool.

THEO

I love Jesus, but I also love it when you spit in my mouth.

MAUD

I completely lack empathy, but I have a rad Tindr account.

THEO

Do you care about me? Do you love me? *Love me.*

MAUD

My heart is horny.

THEO

I like it when you humiliate me.

MAUD

It's *so* depressing when fucking turns into negotiating.

THEO

Fucking implies negotiating.

MAUD

Just take off your clothes bitch.

THEO

Ok. The more disgusting the more I like it.

MAUD

Alright. That's enough.

THEO

Tell me why you're getting married again?

MAUD

Because I need you too much; I know that's what you want to hear –

THEO

Yeah yeah.

MAUD

I met you inside a vacuum of shame . . . but I'd like to meet you on the outside of that vacuum, in normal gravity.

THEO

Ok.

MAUD

Let's just sit and talk. I'll get a bottle of wine from the cellar—

THEO

I'm not in the mood.

MAUD

No?

THEO

Not any more.

MAUD

Theo, I'm sorry.

THEO

You didn't do anything.

MAUD

I don't feel good about this interaction.

THEO

This house is a prism for everything hateful about all of us . . .

MAUD

It's somethin'.

THEO

You're gonna have babies soon.

MAUD

That's the plan.

THEO

Can I be the secret father?

MAUD

No Theo.

THEO

Please?

MAUD

You're not funny.

THEO
I'm serious: let's just fuck without a condom. It would be poetic justice.

MAUD
Justice for what?

THEO
Lots of shit.

MAUD
No Theo.

THEO
Yes Theo.

MAUD
Theo!

THEO
What?!

MAUD
I really miss you—

THEO
Well you really blew it then—

MAUD
So did you.

THEO
Life's a piece of shit.

MAUD
Yup.

THEO
You've tuned out.

MAUD
Yup.

THEO
Because you started feeling vulnerable—

MAUD
You're the devil.

THEO
No, I'm not the devil, I'm just really into your body . . . and that makes you feel ashamed.

MAUD

> I've only been with two guys other than you. I'm guessing you've been with a lot more girls.

THEO

> Sometimes I need . . . to think about girl Y in order to get off with girl X, but then, when I'm with girl Y, I need to think about girl X. That happens to me all the time, shit like that . . .

MAUD

> The light's all silver—

THEO

> Snow—

MAUD

> I like it so much.

THEO

> See ya in the morning.

MAUD

> Wait . . .

THEO

> This isn't worth it anymore.

Exit Theo.

Blackout . . .

Four

The next morning.

Doug at the kitchen table.

Enter Theo.

DOUG
What are you doing up so early ?

THEO
I never went to sleep.

DOUG
Want some coffee?

THEO
I'll have some, sure.

DOUG
Do you have any weed on you?

THEO
Yeah. Use my vape.

Theo hands Doug a device.

DOUG
Thanks.

THEO
Having a rough time?

DOUG
Yes. I am.

THEO
This coffee's terrible.

DOUG
Yeah sorry.

THEO
It's like drinking straight piss.

DOUG
   How's LA?

THEO
   Fine.

DOUG
   Haven't heard any rumblings about new projects lately . . .

THEO
   Because there haven't been any.

DOUG
   Why's that?

THEO
   Nothing's come up. . . . I'm not even sure this coffee; it just might be straight piss.

DOUG
   I can't say I missed having you around the house.

THEO
   Can't say I missed being here.

DOUG
   It hurts your mother how rarely we hear from you—

THEO
   'We'—

DOUG
   So you express your disapproval of me by punishing her?

THEO
   Pretty much.

DOUG
   Pretty selfish.

THEO
   That's me.

DOUG
   Unfortunately.

THEO
   Blah blah blah.

DOUG
   You don't ever seem troubled by the consequences of what you say or do—

THEO
From what you can see—

DOUG
Well what about what I can't see then?

THEO
That's private.

DOUG
You play games with people.

THEO
Do I?

DOUG
What do you call what you do ?

THEO
Nothing: I call it nothing.

DOUG
I'm trying to understand you Theo . . .

THEO
And I'm just trying to sit here and drink this shitty fucking coffee.

DOUG
I guess I find it intimidating to talk to you.

THEO
I don't see why.

DOUG
There's so much clearly going on in your head.

THEO
You have no idea.

DOUG
Yikes.

THEO
Does that bother you?

DOUG
It sets me on edge.

THEO
Good.

DOUG

Or maybe it's all a trick: maybe you're just empty.

THEO

Maybe.

DOUG

What?

THEO

I'm not one of those people who are interested in modeling contemporary ideas about morality.

DOUG

Then what are you interested in?

THEO

I'm tired of trying to convert strangeness into normality; I think I'm ready to stay strange.

DOUG

Great . . .

THEO

Why don't you take another hitty poo?

DOUG

Gladly. . . .

Doug vapes.

DOUG

You know, I didn't like how the father character was portrayed in your last movie.

THEO

Well, no one saw it, so—

DOUG

Some people did—

THEO

A handful at a festival.

DOUG

And I did not like sitting in that audience.

THEO

You spent two hours of your life having to face yourself. Big whoop. I think it was a fairly honest picture of our family. If anything, I was too kind.

DOUG
What do you leave out?

THEO
Stuff.

DOUG
About me?

THEO
In a way.

DOUG
Ok.

THEO
Somehow telling people truth directly just distorts the truth you're trying to convey; so you have to try other approaches.

DOUG
It's funny, the character of the son in your film came off pretty darn well; he's almost flawless.

THEO
Then you weren't paying much attention.

DOUG
I guess not.

THEO
My ears have been ringing ever since I got off the plane. It's driving me crazy.

DOUG
Tug on your earlobes until you hear a crack.

THEO
What'll that do?

DOUG
It opens up the tubes.

THEO
Gross.

DOUG
I'll show you.

THEO
Doug don't touch me.

DOUG

I don't think we've ever physically touched, even to hug.

THEO

Exactly. Let's keep it that way.

DOUG

What did I ever do to you Theo?

THEO

I just naturally dislike weak people.

DOUG

All I've ever done is pay for your expenses: film school, your first feature . . . rent on many occasions.

THEO

You stand to inherit even more than you already have in a few hours, so I think you're doing fine.

DOUG

Do you resent the help?

THEO

I resent the spirit in which it's given. Anyway, thanks for the coffee.

Exit Theo.

Enter Edith.

EDITH

Am I bothering you?

DOUG

Uh . . .

EDITH

Earth to Doug?

DOUG

Hi Edith.

EDITH

I asked if I'm bothering you—?

DOUG

No. Or maybe a little. Doesn't matter.

EDITH
Ok . . . How's your Dad?

DOUG
You know, dying.

EDITH
Oh Doug . . .

DOUG
I'm fine . . .

EDITH
Please let me give you a hug.

DOUG
I'm sorry; I'm just in a foul mood.

EDITH
I understand.

DOUG
Yeah.

EDITH
It's hard.

DOUG
There's supposed to be a blizzard tonight, in which case I've probably seen him for the last time.

EDITH
Then maybe you should go to the hospital this afternoon; you might regret it otherwise.

DOUG
I'm all about regrets: they add a certain fragrance to life, like shadow to sunlight.

EDITH
I don't find your mood right now particularly pleasant.

DOUG
Neither do I.

EDITH
It doesn't feel Christmas, does it?

DOUG
On Christmas Day, my Dad used to get particularly drunk and would inevitably find a reason to whip me with his belt. He'd hit my Mom when she'd try to stop him; also

inevitably. It builds character, a good belting. Of course, it builds the wrong kind of character—but character nonetheless.

EDITH

I wish you'd see a therapist.

DOUG

Why, so you don't have to listen to this shit?

EDITH

Pretty much.

DOUG

Fuck you.

EDITH

Oh that's pleasant.

DOUG

It's my mood.

EDITH

Honestly Doug, you're always like this. Always in these black moods. I'm tired of you using your father's illness as cover.

DOUG

Fine. This is just me. A big fat fucking asshole.

EDITH

I didn't say that.

DOUG

No no: but that's what I am, so.

EDITH

Whatever you say.

DOUG

When I had this house built, Iris was pregnant with Maud, and I had made enough money to not care about my father's point of view. I loved this little piece of woods, how quiet it was, how you couldn't hear any cars; how if you didn't look too far in either direction, it felt a little like living in a very old forest. I had a romanticized idea about family life; about togetherness. I wanted to be a better father than my father was—and I was; I know I was. I had to be. But. Hm. The more successful my father became, the more he went further and further off in the direction of being an outsider . . . of alcoholism. My mom was the opposite, very together, figuring out how to get along . . . before she got cancer . . . I'm sorry—just give me a second—

EDITH
It's ok.

DOUG
Shit.

EDITH
It's really ok.

DOUG
Stop saying that word: 'ok'. You're making me crazy.

EDITH
Sorry.

DOUG
Stop saying that too.

EDITH
Ok.

DOUG
I said stop!

EDITH
Sorry! I mean!

DOUG
You're giving me a headache.

EDITH
Sorry.

DOUG
Edith I'm gonna lose it—

EDITH
Then lose it! I'd rather you let your feelings out than listen to you threaten me with them all day . . .

DOUG
When the girls were little, sometimes I'd just stand outside and watch everyone moving around inside the house—the house that I dreamed up and built—and I'd just weep . . . and then I'd come inside and pretend like nothing unusual was going on. . . . These small spaces of love open up so briefly that it's almost impossible to remember that they were ever there. I just feel so raw. I don't think I've ever felt so raw before.

EDITH
You don't have to be married to me if you don't want to be.

DOUG

Our life together is this kind of fiction that's developed parallel to everything that's real, hasn't it?

EDITH

That's one way to put it.

DOUG

You've never blown me, by the way, not since the first night we met.

EDITH

Is that a complete thought, or do you expect me to draw conclusions for you?

DOUG

The conclusion's built in there, somewhere.

EDITH

I'd be fascinated to hear you articulate it—

DOUG

It's more aesthetic not to.

EDITH

It would have been easier if you had aged into one of those men who give up on erections for good.

DOUG

Easier for both of us—

EDITH

You're emotionally injured and you want attention, someone to stroke your forehead, but at the same time, that's the total opposite of what you want, so you feel like you're losing your mind.

DOUG

A little bit, yeah.

EDITH

Have you ever thought that maybe Iris wasn't as happy with you as you were with her?

DOUG

I've considered it, yes.

EDITH

Because, I'm just saying—

DOUG

That's not 'just saying'—

EDITH

I mean, you act like your first marriage was so incredibly ideal—

DOUG

Real love, no matter how flawed, is always ideal I think—

EDITH

Because you have this intense and very Catholic love of beauty, so when a woman dies before her beauty's gone, it—

DOUG

You're jealous—

EDITH

Of course I'm jealous.

DOUG

It's a very crude thing to be jealous of the dead.

EDITH

Well, that's what I am: a crude, jealous, nagging housewife.

DOUG

But you're not a housewife—

EDITH

But I feel like one, I act like one, I dress like one—what difference does it make that I technically make more money than you do? What difference does it make if I act like your needs—emotional, spiritual, erotic—are the only ones that matter?

DOUG

Mastectomy scars, pregnancy scars, stretch marks and cellulite: who else is gonna love you?

EDITH

You're so full of hatred; it just comes spewing out . . .

DOUG

You're manipulating my emotions . . .

EDITH

It's not hard to figure out why Iris had an affair—

DOUG

Don't—

EDITH

Why she got in the car and drove off a—

DOUG

Hold on—

EDITH

Am I going to far?

DOUG

Way too far.

EDITH

Then I'll stop.

DOUG

What do you want Edith?

EDITH

From you? From life?

DOUG

All of the above.

EDITH

Small things. Achievable things. I'd like to have a better relationship with Clara and Maud. I'd like to retire soon. . . . I don't really need that much more than I have. . . . Life is more complicated than it is long; so if you don't learn to let go of things Doug, then—

DOUG

Then I'll what—

EDITH

Then you'll continue to be really, really confused and unhappy.

DOUG

I want nothing from you but to see you.

EDITH

Needless to say, you're either blind or not looking in the right place . . .

DOUG

There is so much in us that demands a burial . . . so many dead things.

EDITH

If you want sympathy just take it and shut up; or ask for something more sincere—but don't ask me to split the difference between empathy and sympathy, because that's no fun.

DOUG

Married people repeat themselves constantly: open the same wounds, tell the same bad jokes . . .

EDITH

It makes you wonder why there are any married people at all.

DOUG

I want you to be direct with me.

EDITH

I don't see how that's possible.

DOUG

Why not?

EDITH

Because you're sad, desperate, absurd, and unrealistic.

DOUG

That sounded direct.

EDITH

Ok maybe it was.

DOUG

The feeling childhood left me with was one of humiliation.

EDITH

That's the feeling it leaves everyone with.

DOUG

Dad always loved attention. He was a great storyteller. Told wonderful, dirty jokes. He had this big belly laugh. Now he's dying like a stray dog. . . .

EDITH

Painting yourself as the crippled son of a charismatic ego-maniac or whatever—it's clever. . . . It's a big open-mouthed cry for sympathy.

DOUG

It's hard not to want sympathy on the day your father is going to die.

EDITH

Maybe for you . . .

DOUG

Being at church last night brought back terrible memories. I don't know why I went; I don't know why I dragged Maud with me. I just plain don't understand myself sometimes . . . it's . . .

EDITH

Clara thinks I'm a narcissist: she tells me to my face. She told me that I'm manipulative and cold. I read that short story she wrote that was clearly about me; that really made me feel crappy—

DOUG

    Don't listen to Clara—

EDITH

    What if she's right?

DOUG

    Who knows.

EDITH

    Are you even listening to me? You're staring off into space—

DOUG

    We shouldn't be so clinical—all of us—we should just live and let live.

EDITH

    Good luck with that.

DOUG

    I want him to hurry up and die . . .

EDITH

    You really shouldn't say things like that.

DOUG

    I really don't give a shit.

EDITH

    Yeah, I guess I don't either.

Blackout.

Five

Night.

Clara and Doug sit at the kitchen table with a bottle of wine open between them.

CLARA

Are we gonna go to the hospital?

DOUG

Have you looked outside?

CLARA

Honestly, I've never understood why I'm supposed to hate Pop-pop. He always seemed alright to me. He seemed so peaceful this afternoon. He almost seemed wise.

DOUG

I'm not sure if you understand what it was like growing up with him.

CLARA

I think you want to believe that these inexpressible griefs are ennobling, Dad, but I think they're just crippling.

DOUG

Yo, kid—

CLARA

Sorry.

DOUG

I'm not sure why everyone's picking on me on today of all days.

CLARA

I pick on everyone, to be fair.

DOUG

Speaking of you picking on everyone: where's Maud?

CLARA

She's watching a movie upstairs.

DOUG

What about Theo?

CLARA

He's in his room reading. He asked everyone very politely not to fucking disturb him.

DOUG

    Smart guy.

CLARA

    He really understands the correlation between human interaction and misery in this house.

DOUG

    I met Marco and Maud for lunch in the city last week . . .

CLARA

    Pour me another glass—

DOUG

    Is there anyone you approve of Clara?

CLARA

    Not really.

DOUG

    I'm trying to be optimistic about this guy—

CLARA

    I'm trying to be real.

DOUG

    I love you so much Clara—

CLARA

    Please God: no more sentimentality.

DOUG

    Everybody finds me unbearable today.

CLARA

    Sorry, I get ornery when I don't have a working phone.

DOUG

    I know it sucks being stuck in a snowstorm with your family . . . but we all see each other so seldom . . .

CLARA

    When you actually get family-time, all you do is preach about the value of family-time.

DOUG

    Tell me: what would you like to talk about Clara?

CLARA

Anything other than our warmed-over family saga. Like, come on Dad, there's something thoughtless and arrogant about being alone in the room with just your own problems as a companion. I'm so tired of it. Why do you think I take baths all day? Because then I can just be by myself and not think about anything, if I'm lucky enough not to be bothered by anyone, which I rarely am.

DOUG

I hear you.

CLARA

Do you?

DOUG

Yes.

CLARA

I know how to spin words into the air . . . and I'm skillful at understanding the orchestration . . . but the actual melodies are a gift of the universe; in other words, I just say crap Dad—don't look so concerned and hurt.

DOUG

You have an awful lot of rules about how I should interact with you.

CLARA

I'm sorry!

DOUG

Your mother—

CLARA

NO!

DOUG

Fine.

CLARA

I refuse to let myself be plunged into the same emotionally claustrophobic fog that you and Maud have been wandering around in for the last decade and a half.

DOUG

The word "mother" does not imply . . .

CLARA

I said *no*—

DOUG

You wanna talk about emotional atmospheres? Huh? How about you not being so fucking cold to the people around you for a change?

CLARA

Cold isn't the right word: brutal is the word you want.

DOUG

Ok that—*that*—how about you stop being so brutal?

CLARA

It's an interesting practice to harness what's actually going on in your head and try to make other people feel it.

DOUG

Just say what you're feeling then—

CLARA

You should know already—because like—*Dad*—you have a profoundly, profoundly feminine soul; I mean, you've lived this very gender and culture appropriate life, but really inside, you're soft and giving and want to be caressed. A part of you is still in shock that you had this like, gonzo-capitalist father who was vice-president of a bank and drank a lot and wore tailored suits and expensive cologne and had memories from the war and so on; you can't believe you fell into the role of his son, but you've never been able to walk off stage and yank down the curtain either . . . so now that the curtain's falling of its own accord, you're freaked out, not because of grief or even anger—but out of utter confusion. . . . I mean, where do you think Maud got the idea that growing up is about finding a man who will desire her, use her, punish her? She got it from you.

DOUG

Is that where the lecture ends?

CLARA

My notes become illegible after "she got it from you!"

DOUG

Fun.

CLARA

Did it hit home?

DOUG

What do you expect me to say right now?

CLARA

A part you of you is like completely impermeable and impervious. You possess the like the most amazing psychological homeostasis.

DOUG

Sorry but I'm not going to give you a reaction.

CLARA

I'm not testing your reflexes, I'm attempting to communicate.

DOUG

That's a hell of a way to communicate.

CLARA

You know I'm like addicted to dating apps? I just swipe constantly. It's crazy. When no one's around, my phone comes out, almost by magic, by itself. It's sick. It's so sick. Boys, girls. It doesn't matter. I just want. Or I feel like I want. I crave. It's hunger. Or it's just a habit. I've confused habit with hunger. Sick. I really make myself sick. So I'm lashing out, or something; *I'm lashing in.*

DOUG

Now you're making me worried—

CLARA

We're getting off-topic.

DOUG

What was the topic again?

CLARA

I think Pop-pop was also a closet-case, by the way, one in a long line—which is why he was such an alcoholic, and probably why you are too—I mean, you might as well inherit his liquor cabinet after the funeral if I doesn't get to it first—

DOUG

That felt calculated.

CLARA

The snow's really going crazy out there. Do you have any weed in the house?

DOUG

Edith requested that I stop. She got fed up.

CLARA

I'm anxious.

DOUG

Maybe Theo has some.

CLARA

I'm afraid to bother him.

DOUG

Well then I can't help you. Sorry.

CLARA

Dad—

DOUG

What?

CLARA

It's funny—the day you got married to Edith, I had this image flash into my brain of you, with a wedding dress hiked over your shoulders, being fucked by a strap-on-wearing Edith. I almost burst out laughing during the "to have and to hold" part of the ceremony. The more I tried not to think about it, the funnier it became.

DOUG

You didn't want us to get married.

CLARA

Not really.

DOUG

I'm aware it doesn't seem that way a lot of the time, but Edith and I are happy together.

CLARA

I really don't care either way. I'm getting a headache. I wish you had weed Dad.

DOUG

So do I.

CLARA

I don't get how my life can feel meaningless and stressful at the same time. Stress should mean something meaningful is at risk; but I don't feel like that's the case with me.

DOUG

I worry so much about you and your sister.

CLARA

You worry we're damaged goods—

DOUG

That's not what I mean.

CLARA

Yes it is.

DOUG

I want you to be happy.

CLARA

I'm not gonna be happy, that's not in the cards.

DOUG

Why not?

CLARA

The only way to bind up pain is with pain.

DOUG

I'm not sure what you mean.

CLARA

Neither am I.

DOUG

Have you talked to Theo much?

CLARA

A little, why?

DOUG

Just wondering.

CLARA

I don't really know Theo anymore and I'm not sure I want to.

DOUG

I get it.

CLARA

No, you don't get it.

DOUG

Ok, I don't get it then.

CLARA

Dad—

DOUG

What?

CLARA

Never mind.

Enter Maud.

DOUG

Hi Maud. Ok girls, I'm going to bed.

CLARA

Goodnight night.

MAUD

Love you.

DOUG

> Love you too. G'night.

Exit Doug.

MAUD

> I couldn't stop crying in the shower just now, and then the hot water ran out and I stayed in there, crying until my hands started turning blue—

CLARA

> Why?

MAUD

> I don't know.

CLARA

> Uh yeah. So.

MAUD

> I can't take this; I really can't.

CLARA

> Take what?

MAUD

> Nevermind.

CLARA

> Oh shit.

MAUD

> What?

CLARA

> I just realized something.

MAUD

> What are you talking about!

CLARA

> Something just clicked into place for me. That's all.

MAUD

> What!

CLARA

> I don't wanna say it.

MAUD

> Sure you do—

CLARA

Uh, no. Nope. No.

MAUD

Was it something Dad said?

CLARA

Not at all—

MAUD

Something I said?

CLARA

You didn't sleep last night did you?

MAUD

No.

CLARA

Why?

MAUD

I had a lot on my mind.

CLARA

Is that it?

MAUD

Yes, what else would there be?

CLARA

Um.

MAUD

What?

CLARA

It's like I've seen the light—

MAUD

What are you talking about?

CLARA

Something very disquieting.

MAUD

Ok . . .

CLARA

You shouldn't marry Marco if you feel this way about about Theo.

MAUD

    Holy fucking shit Clara—*what*—?

CLARA

    There's no need to be so defensive.

MAUD

    You're just making shit up.

CLARA

    No: I speak from experience . . .

MAUD

    I'm confused . . .

CLARA

    Of course you are. . . .

MAUD

    I need a drink . . . *What?*

CLARA

    This whole time . . . amazing . . . completely amazing . . .

MAUD

    What?! I'm gonna kill you!

CLARA

    Does Theo make you stick your finger in his ass too?

MAUD

    Excuse me?

CLARA

    I'm asking—

MAUD

    Oh my God—

CLARA

    But maybe he's different with you . . .

MAUD

    Oh my God . . .

CLARA

    I have to hand it to him . . . it's pretty slick . . .

MAUD

    Please tell me you're joking—

CLARA

I, uh, I wish I was.

MAUD

I feel . . .

CLARA

Yeah.

MAUD

This is crazytown.

CLARA

Maud, breathe. It's just sex.

MAUD

What's wrong with you?

CLARA

Maud I didn't know . . . . I had no idea . . .

MAUD

Sick sick sick sick sick.

CLARA

Relax. Breathe.

A phone rings offstage. Doug's voice is heard answering.

MAUD

I can't take this.

CLARA

Poor Pop-pop . . .

Enter Doug.

DOUG

It's over.

CLARA

We know.

DOUG

It's all over . . .

CLARA

I'm sorry Dad.

A pause.

Maud stands up, as if disoriented, and goes to the window.

MAUD
I see her out there.

CLARA
Who?

MAUD
She's walking towards the house.

DOUG
Maud, are you alright?

MAUD
Mom didn't die; you were lying.

DOUG
Maud—

MAUD
She's been out there this whole time . . . waiting for us to call her back.

CLARA
Yo, Maud—snap out of it—

MAUD
She looks so happy—

DOUG
Kiddo—

MAUD
Dad, you were lying . . . everyone's been lying . . .

DOUG
Maud, you're making me worried—

MAUD
Mother, I belong to you; I belong to you. I've been waiting for so long—*your daughter* –

CLARA
Hello? Yo?

MAUD
I've been waiting. And here you are . . .

DOUG
   Maud . . .

MAUD
   Here you are . . .

                            Blackout.

Quartet

"Get thee a good husband, and use him as he uses thee."

—Shakespeare

Quartet premiered at Ty's Loft in Greenpoint, Brooklyn in June of 2021. This version of the script premiered at a private loft in Tribeca in September of 2022. Both productions had the following cast:

Nick: Christian Stevenson
Jay: Connor Hall
Elizabeth: Eliza Vann
Ellie: Katie Kane

Directed by Matthew Gasda

Cast of Characters

All characters late 20s
Jay: shambolic, aristocratic alcoholic, about to marry Elizabeth
Elizabeth: a classic WASP of good breeding and elegant self presentation, a bit uptight
Ellie: a little more of a basic bitch than Elizabeth, corporate striver, knows how to have fun
Nick: young lawyer, former college student, Ellie's longtime boyfriend, a bit of wildcard in social situations

Setting

An upscale, modern apartment. Night. ELIZABETH and JAY, NICK and ELLIE, two couples, drink cocktails. They're mid-conversation. It's the night before Elizabeth and Jay's rehearsal dinner.

One

JAY

Anyway, I think it's just jealousy on his part.

NICK

Still, it fucking bothers me. Like, *damn*. . . . the fact that he said it—

JAY	**ELIZABETH**
He's a narcissist dude—	
	Just like you my love—

there's nothing you can do about it.

ELLIE

I would just let it go Nick.

NICK

I just can't seem to set my expectations of people low enough to not get disappointed.

ELIZABETH

Join the club.

JAY

I'm drunk by the way.

ELIZABETH

See what I mean?

ELLIE

Humans are gonna human.

NICK

Yup.

JAY

I've been drinking since lunch.

ELLIE

Geeze man.

JAY

Nah; it's good, it's good; I'm loose—

ELIZABETH

It's a problem right?

ELLIE

Do you wanna talk about it Jay?

JAY

Fuck you in the face Ellie.

ELLIE

I guess that's a 'no.'

ELIZABETH

He's barbaric, I'm sorry.

ELLIE

No it's alright; I'm used to being treated this way—

NICK

That's not fair—come on—

JAY

I just broke wind a little if anyone smells what the rock is cooking.

ELIZABETH	ELLIE
Ew Jay that's gross . . .	Oh it's awful—

NICK

Mm. Fruity.

JAY

With hints of lemon grass and orange peel.

NICK

Speaking of gas—

ELLIE

Oh no—

NICK

My grandfather told me this story—

ELLIE

Can we not have story time?

NICK

Can you not interrupt me?

ELLIE

Never mind.

NICK

Anyway, when my grandfather was in college, his apartment was attacked by bedbugs, but he was too poor to afford an exterminator, so—

ELIZABETH

Where is this going?

JAY

    Shhhhhhhhhh.

NICK

    So—after months and months of not sleeping, he gives in and calls the exterminator and, like, negotiates a deal—uses all his savings, whatever whatever—and the apartment gets fumigated . . . except the exterminator forgets to the tell the family next door that there's a fumigation going on . . .

JAY

    Oh shit—

NICK

    And the fumes . . . kill the neighbors' baby.

JAY

    One less mouth to feed . . . am I right?

ELIZABETH

    Is that a true story?

NICK

    Yeah.

ELIZABETH

    It's disturbing.

NICK

    Sorry.

ELIZABETH

    Like, really.

ELLIE

    Can I open a window?

JAY

    Go for it.

NICK

    When did you guys move into the Playboy Condo?

ELIZABETH

    Like a month ago.

NICK

    It's fucking dope.

JAY

    Thanks man.

ELLIE

You're renting?

JAY

Unfortunately.

NICK

Have your parents buy it—

ELLIE

Nick—

JAY

I don't wanna ask bro; it's uncomfortable.

NICK

It's *thirty* seconds of passive income for them.

JAY

Hey buddy, can we not talk about my family's finances?

ELLIE

You're being rude Nick.

NICK

I lack filter. Robot needs filter.

ELIZABETH

Please don't chew on my pillows . . .

NICK

Would you prefer if I gently licked them, like a vulva?

ELIZABETH

No I wouldn't.

ELLIE

Drop the pillow Nick—

NICK

When I was in middle school, I used to fuck pillows all the time—make a little hole— *wham!*

ELIZABETH

It's not too late to pick another best man . . . like seriously—

ELLIE

Let's just hope he's getting it out of his system.

ELIZABETH	JAY
	Nick is my guy—
I'm very nervous.	
	right Nick?

NICK
Right. Dap it.

JAY
That's true love right there baby.

ELIZABETH
I'm so concerned.

JAY
Babe, tomorrow's gonna be so much fun and so chill—

ELIZABETH
I remain unconvinced.

ELLIE
Honestly, I'm really happy for the two of you! It's so exciting!

JAY
I just hope I don't let one *rip* while we're standing at the altar—

ELLIE
I think you'll be alright Jay.

JAY
Our Lady of the Shart Cathedral—

NICK
I'm gonna practice my speech—

ELLIE
Oh no—

JAY
Yes king—

NICK
Four score and seven beers ago . . . our bride-to-be Elizabeth, fulfilling a lifelong dream, met the richest man at Dartmouth . . . when a mysterious and handsome . . . penis . . . pushed its way into her mouth in the basement of a frat house –

ELLIE
Nick, shut the fuck up, for God's sake.

NICK

Hey it's a free country.

ELIZABETH

I'm just gonna pretend I'm okay with all of this.

ELLIE

We can't let them get too much momentum—

NICK

Speaking of, I'm just wondering if we're gonna do this or not.

JAY

Someone's gotta start taking off their clothes—right?

ELIZABETH	ELLIE
I'm not gonna volunteer . . .	I thought
And like, the way you guys are acting—	we agreed it was only an option, not like a thing that had to happen one hundred percent.

NICK

What's wrong with the way we're acting?!

ELLIE

Just about everything.

JAY	NICK
Get the fuck outta here!	Yeah! We're gentlemen.

ELIZABETH

Neither of you can keep it together.

JAY

Liz, you have no idea how hard I'm trying right now—please—

ELIZABETH

Jay that's uh . . .

JAY

That's uh what?

ELIZABETH

No comment.

JAY

Not counting cocaine for a second, all the worst moments of my life involve gin.

ELLIE

So then why drink it?

ELIZABETH

JAY
Because—*Ellie*—
It wants me to!
You see—the point—
of doing the same thing over and over
is to convince yourself that the bad
behavior is normal!

Relax
relax—
relax—
relax—
relax—

NICK
It is normal—

ELLIE
We should just ignore them.

NICK
Yes, you can do so by making out please.

JAY
Or skip right to scissoring—

ELLIE
I don't think that's going to happen.

NICK
Oh my god why not?

ELIZABETH
You two don't deserve it.

NICK
Oh come on!

JAY
Honestly, I really feel like you and Ellie are dying to indulge your lesbian tendencies.

ELLIE
They watch way too much porn . . .

ELIZABETH
Oh, Jay, my friend, do you really want
to start talking about repressed
homoerotic tendencies?

JAY
No thanks.

ELIZABETH
Exactly.

ELLIE
Boom.

NICK

    Can we please put on some music?

JAY

    Absolutely we can.

Jay picks something out.

ELIZABETH

    I'm anxious.

JAY

    Don't overthink it.

ELIZABETH

    That's not in my nature.

JAY

    Change your nature then honey.

ELIZABETH

    Only if you go first.

JAY

    If I could, I would—trust me.

ELIZABETH

    Yeah . . .

NICK

    You know—this is all very boomer: cocktails and living rooms, vague couple swapping vibes . . .

JAY

    That sounds about right.

ELIZABETH

    Ellie—how's your new job?

NICK

    She wants to quit.

ELLIE

    That's not entirely true.

JAY

    What do you do again?

ELLIE

    Consulting.

JAY
> So you hate your life—

ELLIE
> Sometimes, yeah—

JAY
> Are you good at it? Do you slay? Do you kill it?

ELLIE
> I mean—are you good at your job Jay?

JAY
> Hell no.

ELLIE
> Does that bother you—?

JAY
> Hell no. My whole life is sitting on the pot and hoping no one asks me to get off it.

ELLIE
> Speaking of sitting on the pot, where's the bathroom?

ELIZABETH
> Next to the bedroom, down the hall.

ELLIE
> Thank you.

Exit Ellie.

NICK
> I think we're gonna break up. Don't say anything.

Jay laughs.

ELIZABETH
> Seriously?

NICK
> Yeah.

ELIZABETH
> Does Ellie know this?

NICK
> No, she doesn't.

ELIZABETH

    You're an asshole.

NICK

    I know.

JAY

    What's the deal?

NICK

    I feel trapped. I want explore new people.

JAY

    Just let her peg you: you'll love it . . .

ELIZABETH

    She obviously wants to get married. Is that what's scaring you off?

NICK

    Next question.

ELIZABETH

    No one wants to be a prom-date forever. Women want something real.

NICK

    You sound like my mom.

ELIZABETH

    I bet I do.

NICK

    But I don't wanna fuck my mom.

ELIZABETH

    Are you sure about that?

NICK

    Look—Liz—neither of you knows what it's like; I'm constantly being monitored . . . I mean, it's awful. I'm totally doing the dance—

ELIZABETH

    You're such a retard.

Ellie returns.

JAY

    How was your dump Ellie?

ELLIE

    You know Jay, it wasn't bad at all.

JAY
> Good to hear.

ELLIE
> The candles were a nice touch.

JAY
> That's all Liz.

ELLIE
> Thanks Liz. Jay is this drink for me?

JAY
> It is.

ELLIE
> Dude this is so strong.

JAY
> I can't taste the alcohol unless it's like all alcohol. Cheers everyone.

NICK
> Make eye contact!

ELIZABETH
> Yeah yeah.

ELLIE
> What shows have you guys been watching?

JAY
> Uhhhhhhh. . . .

NICK
> We love that British thing—I never remember the title—but it's good—

ELIZABETH
> I've made a vow not to talk about TV in social situations—actually—

NICK
> Whoops—

ELLIE
> That's a little judgy . . .

JAY
> I mean, have you met her?

ELIZABETH
> I just prefer books. . . . I mean I have literature degree, right? Why not use it?

NICK

She said it!

JAY

Everybody's got to take a shot now!

ELIZABETH

Do I really bring that up every time we get together?

ELLIE

Honestly, yeah, you do.

ELIZABETH

Fuck me.

JAY

Everybody's got their insecurities baby, don't let it get you down—

ELIZABETH

I guess I just feel like I should be doing more interesting things with my life—

NICK

You're super successful Lizzy.

ELIZABETH

But there's zero creativity.

NICK

Who says there has to be creativity?

ELIZABETH

My inner voice.

NICK

Just take pills; it'll go away.

ELIZABETH

I do, that's the problem.

JAY

I tell her to just take double what the bottle says is safe. Works for me!

ELLIE

Joking?

ELIZABETH

Sadly none of his cries for help are jokes.

JAY

Admittedly, my whole life is an attempt to replace an acute anxiety with passive anxiety.

ELLIE
  You need a good therapist.

JAY
  I have two: a psychologist and a psychiatrist.

ELIZABETH
  It's true. He's always on the phone with one or the other.

JAY
  Allan and Frank are my friends!

ELIZABETH
  Those are pretty expensive friends.

JAY
  Honestly, disregarding Frank for a second, Allen is a bargain—

NICK
  Are these vodka shots?

JAY
  Yeah, good vodka too.

NICK
  Can't beat expensive . . .

JAY
  Unfortunately, you cannot . . . You know, honestly—I'd give my money away except for the fact that Liz would leave me immediately—

ELLIE
  Woah now.

ELIZABETH
  I don't think you understand the pressure of living month to month Jay—

NICK
  Do you Liz?

ELIZABETH
  No. Which is why I think it's harder than it looks.

JAY
  I also honestly—trigger warning—hate poor people.

ELLIE
  Ok Jay . . .

JAY

Like—I secretly plan genocides for homeless people in my head—just like—why not put them out of their misery?

NICK

Wow that's so wrong it's funny . . .

ELIZABETH

Honey, your life would be so much easier if you never shared your real thoughts with anyone, including me.

JAY

Is it too late to get a pre-nup?

NICK

No—

ELIZABETH

Ok that's enough.

NICK

Jay, did Jon really say that about me?

JAY

Yeah dude. I'm sorry.

NICK

Yo! Where does he get off?!

JAY

He's changed . . . ever since he's started dating what's her face—?

ELLIE

Alina.

NICK

How do you know that? She's not even your friend.

ELLIE

Instagram stories: she's very active.

ELIZABETH

What does she post?

ELLIE

I dunno, some bullshit. Like, it's very curated. So you know it's rotten to the core. Also I think she's cheating on him?

JAY

Whoa, how do you know that?

ELLIE
You can just tell sometimes with these bitches. It's like –

ELIZABETH
You just can.

NICK
Fuck people.

JAY
You guys are the last people I'm friends with from college.

NICK
Ditto.

JAY
They drop like flies.

ELLIE
College was fun though.

ELIZABETH
Was it?

ELLIE
I mean, it was for me.

NICK
I wish I didn't miss it so much personally—

ELLIE
I miss your pre-law school body in all its glory.

NICK
When I was still in soccer shape baby—

JAY
I've got these little knobby handles beginning to form under my ribs. It's creepy.

ELIZABETH
I feel like I'm making love with a jelly doughnut sometimes.

NICK
Gotta go paleo dude.

JAY
I've thought about it. But how does alcohol fit in?

NICK
I mean, the idea is to get your metabolism to a place where it can handle a little fun.

JAY

    I'm down; I'm just not very disciplined.

ELIZABETH

    Jay eats cake for breakfast.

NICK

    You'll never make it to the Singularity eating like that bro.

ELIZABETH

    Jay will be lucky to make it to tomorrow—

JAY

    Nick needs to train me—- like take me up to the mountains and make me chop wood and yell at me and feed me raw venison—yum yum yum—

ELLIE

    That sounds so gay.

ELIZABETH

    Doesn't it?

JAY

    Whatever.

ELIZABETH

    Nick, I realize you're kind of, um, simultaneously a twink and a chad—

NICK

    What's a twink?

ELLIE

    Really?

NICK

    I'm gonna assume it's a compliment?

ELIZABETH

    You can choose to believe that.

ELLIE

    It's getting silly.

JAY

    What else is it supposed to get?

ELLIE

    Well, we could have an actual, like, sophisticated conversation.

ELIZABETH	NICK
Good luck.	What's that supposed to mean?

JAY
>Yeah. What is that supposed to mean?

ELLIE
>It means that we could like discuss, um—

ELIZABETH
>Actual ideas—

JAY
>Like who has the biggest dick?

ELIZABETH
>You're pathetic.

JAY
>Ok don't marry me then.

ELIZABETH
>Maybe I won't.

JAY
>Great.

ELLIE
>Maybe we should watch a movie.

ELIZABETH
>Are we having a sleep over?

ELLIE
>That would actually be fun.

ELIZABETH
>Eh.

ELLIE
>Maybe we should just do it—

ELIZABETH
>I'm not sure if I'm in the mood . . .

ELLIE
>Aw –

ELIZABETH
>I just can't relax. I'm sorry everyone. I'm trying.

ELLIE

Don't put pressure on yourself.

NICK

We should do a four-way massage . . .

ELLIE

Have you ever—before?

ELIZABETH

Just once with this couple we met on a cruise-ship.

NICK

You went on a cruise?

JAY

For her birthday last year.

NICK

I'm not old enough to accept that my friends meet swingers on cruises. Did you lock eyes in the Conga line?

JAY

Funny you ask—

ELLIE

Did you just swap—or?

JAY

Strictly swapping.

NICK

How much older are we talking exactly?

ELIZABETH

I dunno, forties.

ELLIE

That's not bad.

ELIZABETH

Why do people lose all attractiveness after forty? It's kinda fucked up to think that we're sexual commodities with exponentially decreasing worth.

ELLIE

I guess that's why it's important to develop other kinds of values besides sex as you get older—

NICK

Like money.

ELLIE
    No, asshole.

JAY
    I challenge either of you to name one other so-called value—other than sex or
    money—that has any real power in the world.

      ELIZABETH   ELLIE
Uh, like unconditional love.

                                                   Truth?

Honesty.

                                                   Kindness?

Conviction.

                                                   Faith?

JAY
    Boners—

NICK
    Porn—

JAY
    Beer—

NICK
    Sports—

JAY
    Video games—

ELLIE
    This is hopeless.

ELIZABETH
    I sound very old fashioned don't I?

NICK
    Liz, once you accept that we live in a simulation, you'll be much happier.

ELIZABETH
    I'm sure.

JAY
    I think it's time to meet our friend Mr. Cocaine. I don't know how else to save the
    evening.

ELIZABETH
    Jay, put it away.

JAY

　My cock or the coke?

ELIZABETH

　Well, your cock isn't out . . .

JAY

　But—in my mind it's out. My mental cock is throbbing.

ELIZABETH

　Oh my god Jay . . . just put the coke away.

JAY

　Fucking Nazi.

ELIZABETH

　Jay . . .

JAY

　Whatever.

NICK

Does anyone ever think about how . . .
there's no difference between dead
people and people who have yet to
be born?
It's crazy right ?
Like?

ELLIE

Nick
you need to stop smoking so
much weed.

JAY

　I think I'm losing my hair.

ELIZABETH

　This is one of his paranoid delusions—

ELLIE

　Are you afraid you'll be unloveable bald?

JAY

　No no—I'm already unloveable; I'm just a narcissist.

ELLIE

　Fair enough.

ELIZABETH

　What's the female equivalent of going bald? Getting fat? Wrinkles? Both? Either? Just
　getting pregnant?

ELLIE
Any deviation from the ideal of adolescent fucktoy is our equivalent of going bald.

NICK
Are men really that shitty?

ELIZABETH
I mean.

NICK
Come on. Like take us for instance—

JAY
We're just having fun—

NICK
Because we're fun as fuck—

ELIZABETH
I think more than fun, I'd like sanity, but maybe that's just me.

NICK
'Just you'—Liz you're a sad, joyless person. You're the least interesting person here.

ELIZABETH
Thanks Nick.

JAY   ELLIE
Speaking truth to power my guy.   Holy shit guys.

ELIZABETH
In a way, the savagery feels good.

NICK
Thank you.

JAY
She needed to hear it from someone.

ELIZABETH
Uhuh.

ELLIE
Maybe we should go? I feel like—I dunno—feels like the vibe is off.

JAY
Hold on.

ELLIE
What?

JAY

Life would just be so much more interesting if we actually followed through on this.

ELLIE

Well that's probably true.

NICK

I'm gonna pour myself another drink and relax. Here, Liz why don't you sit next to Ellie—

ELIZABETH

Nick, chill.

NICK

I'm so chill.

ELLIE

Oh god, Jay—why are you turning down the lights?

JAY

Because Ellie, it's time.

Gradual blackout.

Two

A few months later. Enter Nick and Elizabeth, getting dressed. Nick kisses Elizabeth.

ELIZABETH
Why are you in such a hurry to go?

NICK
Fleeing the crime scene obviously.

ELIZABETH
Relax. We're fine. Papa's not gonna be home for awhile.

NICK
It's his emotional not physical proximity—

ELIZABETH
Let's enjoy this while we have it.

NICK
No, I think this has gotta stop.

ELIZABETH
Porquoi?

NICK
It's just not worth it.

ELIZABETH
Worth what?

NICK
The moral warping effect.

ELIZABETH
Personally, I'm fine with that.

NICK
Maybe I'm realizing that I don't want to completely fuck up my life.

ELIZABETH
Maybe I'm realizing that I do.

NICK
Well I'm not going down with the ship.

ELIZABETH
You may not have a choice.

NICK

Oh great.

ELIZABETH

I'm just really turned on by you. You make me so wet.

NICK

I'm not sure why.

ELIZABETH

Because you're so selfish. Why do you like me?

NICK

Because you're so empty.

ELIZABETH

Sometimes I wonder if Ellie and Jay kept hooking up too—

NICK

I don't feel like they had much chemistry.

ELIZABETH

Did Ellie tell you that?

NICK

Yeah she did.

ELIZABETH

I don't think you like the perversity you're starting to recognize in yourself—

NICK

No, I don't.

ELIZABETH

Or the fact that that perversity is bound up with feelings . . .

NICK

Which I don't want to have!

ELIZABETH

Just make them go away with that magic wand of yours.

NICK

Hey hey hey—not right now. . . .

ELIZABETH

Alright.

NICK

Knock knock—

ELIZABETH
No—

NICK
Who's there? Knock knock—

ELIZABETH
No Nick.

NICK
Ok.

ELIZABETH
Why are you looking at me like that?

NICK
I don't know why I keep expecting you to snap out of it.

ELIZABETH
Out of what?

NICK
The trance of your life.

ELIZABETH
Ah.

NICK
Liz: just say it . . .

ELIZABETH
What?

NICK
Say you love his money.

ELIZABETH
No.

NICK
No, come on: say you love his pesticide, his carcinogen, his hope-we-don't-attract-a-class-action-lawsuit money—

ELIZABETH
I like being taken care of—ok?

NICK
You made a big mistake . . .

ELIZABETH
It's not that simple—

NICK

    Which is why you texted me—

ELIZABETH

    He was passed out and it was our wedding night and I was sad—

NICK

    Because you were in checkmate—

ELIZABETH

    It's going to be an open marriage.

NICK

    Does Jay know that?

ELIZABETH

    He'll figure it out.

NICK

    He's a jealous person.

ELIZABETH

    But he's also an alcoholic with a wandering eye who has an easier time getting it up with random women than his partner—

NICK

    Or men—

ELIZABETH

    Do you know that for a fact?

NICK

    Definitely in college a little bit. Like some blow jobs?

ELIZABETH

    Did you two—?

NICK

    Uh, no. Did you enjoy Ellie making you squirt that night?

ELIZABETH

    Party trick. Are you hard again? I'm still horny.

NICK

    I'm a slow re-loader.

ELIZABETH

    I want your dick in me Nick.

NICK

    My dick is done for the day.

ELIZABETH
>Let's have a baby!

NICK
>No.

ELIZABETH
>You were never gonna break up with her—

NICK
>Of course not.

ELIZABETH
>Coward.

NICK
>Ok—even I just said fuck it and actually broke up with her . . . I would just get in another relationship exactly like the one I'm in now—

ELIZABETH
>I'm jealous of her Nick.

NICK
>Don't be—

ELIZABETH
>Really, really fucking jealous—

NICK
>You wanted me to marry this person! Don't you remember?

ELIZABETH
>I hadn't discovered how much I liked having sex with you yet . . . or realized how shitty she was—

NICK
>Why do you say she's shitty?

ELIZABETH
>No, it was the way she touched me that night—

NICK
>Oh.

ELIZABETH
>Like I was her doll—

NICK
>Sounds about right.

ELIZABETH

I just wanna understand what you get out of it.

NICK

It's a mutual security pact—

ELIZABETH

Ok.

NICK

That's it.

ELIZABETH

Good for you.

NICK

What most people want is a mediocre person who will reliably tell them that they're special, right?

ELIZABETH

Nick. I just want to lick your ass; I want to excite you. Please. I just want to stop thinking, stop analyzing . . .

NICK

Oh man Liz . . . just gimme some space here—ok? I'm serious—Come on—

ELIZABETH

What are your fantasies? Tell me –

NICK

Not to be responsible for anyone else's happiness.

ELIZABETH

Nick you're no fun. What if we watched porn together?

NICK

Wouldn't help. Sorry.

ELIZABETH

It's fine, I'll just find someone else.

NICK

Seriously?

ELIZABETH

I need to find a way of restoring some of the energy Jay drains from me day in and day out.

NICK

Maybe you shouldn't have quit your job.

ELIZABETH

Why should I work? There's absolutely no need. I'd rather sit at home and read.

NICK

Sounds nice.

ELIZABETH

You hate him –

NICK

I hate how much was given to him right up front.

ELIZABETH

So this is class revenge?

NICK

It's just not fair that his life is so much easier than mine.

ELIZABETH

Jay's life is far from easy.

NICK

How can that possibly be true?

ELIZABETH

Well his brother committed suicide. We can start there.

NICK

I thought it was a car accident?

ELIZABETH

Quote unquote.

NICK

Damn. What else?

ELIZABETH

His mother is severely borderline.

NICK

Who isn't? Next?

ELIZABETH

His father's an asshole.

NICK

Obviously. What else?

ELIZABETH

This is kind of undignified.

NICK

Exactly. What else?

ELIZABETH

He has a small cock.

NICK

I know that one already. Obviously.

ELIZABETH

Oh right.

NICK

What else?

ELIZABETH

He's onto his fourth stepmom.

NICK

What else?

ELIZABETH

He's aware that he's not intelligent enough to succeed without his family connections—

NICK

What else babe?

ELIZABETH

His new wife is banging his best friend—

NICK

He doesn't know that one yet. What else?!

ELIZABETH

And yet it counts. Are you satisfied yet?

NICK

I feel like this is a smokescreen for an even more messed up Jay—

ELIZABETH

You'll never know.

NICK

It bothers me that he always splits drinks with me when we go out to bars; like why can't he just pay—like—

ELIZABETH

He would if you asked.

NICK

I'm never gonna ask.

ELIZABETH
Can I suck your cock? I don't care if it's soft.

NICK
It's not gonna happen . . .

ELIZABETH
Do you let Ellie?

NICK
Once in awhile, just enough that she feels valued.

ELIZABETH
Why are you such an asshole?

NICK
Why do you have such fucking expensive pillows?! And why do I wanna hump them all the time? This is absurd. I need to go. I wanna go.

ELIZABETH
You're upsetting me—

NICK
Hey—

ELIZABETH
Why are you with her?

NICK
See, I don't like these little flare-ups of anguish; they really disturb me—

ELIZABETH
What? Is it getting too real for you?

NICK
Look, Liz, I don't think I can deal with your episodes anymore—

ELIZABETH
You sound like me talking to Jay—

NICK
I just—

ELIZABETH
What? You don't like having to watch someone else suffer? You don't like finding out that your choices have consequences?

NICK

> Don't you think I'm suffering too? Listen—Sometimes after we're together . . . I just go home and lay on the floor . . . because I'm too destroyed to do anything else . . . . . . and Ellie thinks it's her fault . . . fuck. . . .

ELIZABETH

> I don't like it when people cry.

NICK

> It's fine, I can just stop.

ELIZABETH

> Thanks.

NICK

> The weird part is . . . I feel like I deserve emotional punishment from people to the point where I almost begin to crave it . . .

ELIZABETH

> God sometimes I wish I was man.

NICK

> You'd be good at it.

ELIZABETH

> I'd love to ram you really hard: uh uh uh—

NICK

> This is dumb. We're dumb.

ELIZABETH

> Idealizing someone is essentially a form of cruelty I think.

NICK

> Do you wanna hear a song I wrote? It's about us.

ELIZABETH

> I prefer not to—no.

ELIZABETH	NICK
Let's be together. Let's go somewhere. Let's get out of the city—Let's just forget about everything—	I'm a little tea pot short and stout—here is—my handle . . . here is my—

ELIZABETH

> This all feels so unintentional, so animal . . . random.

NICK

> Do you remember the look on Jay's face while he watched us fuck?

ELIZABETH
I wasn't paying attention.

NICK
Yes you were. Did you hide my shoes while I was getting dressed?

ELIZABETH
I want to explore you—

NICK
Is my penis being held hostage?

ELIZABETH
It is, yes.

NICK
They're under the couch aren't they?

ELIZABETH
No, don't look, that'll ruin it.

NICK
I have to go back to work.

ELIZABETH
You're 'working from home today'.

NICK
I just want to leave.

ELIZABETH
Please don't cut me off—

NICK
We're friends—remember?

ELIZABETH
No I mean—

NICK
I know what you mean.

ELIZABETH
Nick! Do you want to have a baby?

NICK
Not with you.

ELIZABETH
Fuck you! You don't get it!

NICK
Get what?!

ELIZABETH
You're not even my type!

NICK
Thanks.

ELIZABETH
There's nothing sophisticated or interesting about you. In a vacuum, I wouldn't even notice you. You wouldn't exist. But I'm too vain not to enjoy the attention of this eager little boy, this horny teenager. . . . You actually make me feel old Nick, like an old woman . . . sometimes I can't believe we're the same age . . . or live in the same universe. . . . I've somehow converted all of my self-love into love for you like a currency exchange—and I keep expecting you to give the money back at a higher value, but you don't. . . . I mean, I think I just have to admit that I've fallen for the wrong person . . . out of boredom . . . or just sheer indifference—a person with no creativity or insight or grace or . . . like you've basically already admitted . . . no class.

NICK
How comes you never acknowledge your nose job by the way?

ELIZABETH
Here have your shoes—

NICK
You know I know who paid for it—

ELIZABETH
Go. Get out of here.

NICK
Never. I'm just gonna sit here until he comes home and we can duke it out like proper gentlemen.

ELIZABETH
You're too much of a coward.

NICK
I know, I know: it's what makes me *me*.

ELIZABETH
I wouldn't mind being fought over though. Honestly.

NICK
I know you wouldn't.

ELIZABETH
It's what makes me *me*.

NICK
Shoes are going on.

ELIZABETH
It's been a time.

NICK
Yup.

ELIZABETH
Actually, please don't go . . .

NICK
There was um . . . there was a moment about two years—I don't even know if I can explain it really—when Ellie got way too drunk at a party . . . like, serious alcohol poisoning—like she didn't eat enough or something . . . maybe got slipped something—I dunno. . . . and um . . . there were just, like, a few minutes where I really thought, like, she's gonna die on the bathroom floor; she's gonna die in my arms—and . . . and . . . I just remember it dawning on me that this is what love is: it's just the shock . . . that travels down the line from death . . .

ELIZABETH
You're hurting me.

NICK
Take more Prozac—or have you built up a tolerance?

ELIZABETH
Nick, I'm in so much pain . . .

NICK
Sounds like you should go to one of those silent meditation retreats where you just stare at a wall for ten days until you start seeing your spirit animal or whatever.

ELIZABETH
Ok goodbye.

Exit Nick. Elizabeth tidies up the apartment in distress.

Three

The apartment. Afternoon. Sometime in the future. Ellie and Jay sit pensively on the couch.

ELLIE

You're making me more anxious than I already am . . . don't hold my hand.

JAY

Are you sure you're not into revenge sex?

ELLIE

No, I'm not attracted to you.

JAY

Really?

ELLIE

Jay . . .

JAY

You know, under the surface, I'm less terrible—as a person.

ELLIE

I'm sure, actually. But.

JAY

What?

ELLIE

This really isn't about either of us; it's just about gaining some clarity.

JAY

More like: getting back control—

ELLIE

I say clarity; you say control.

JAY

Potato, po-tot-toh.

ELLIE

I don't even know if I'm angry about it anymore.

JAY

I just want to exploit the moral high ground while I have it.

ELLIE	JAY
This is going to be a conversation Jay.	
Not a—	Sure.
I dunno –	Whatever.

ELLIE

Do you really think that when the door opens all the things you planned to say will come out the way you imagined them?

JAY

I have no idea.

ELLIE

What if he's not with her? What if they change their plans?

JAY

Then we look like weirdos.

ELLIE

She's gonna flip things around on you for reading her messages . . .

JAY

So what? I had a good reason to be reading them as it turns out –

ELLIE

What about the idea of privacy being sacred?

JAY

Nah. That's silly.

ELLIE

Oh is it? Can I read through your phone then?

JAY

Stop judging me.

ELLIE

I don't really have any deep opinions about you Jay. You're my boyfriend's buddy. That's our relationship.

JAY

And I fucked you that time too—

ELLIE

If you wanna call it that—

JAY

Mean . . .

ELLIE

> Stop trying to hold my hand!

JAY

> Geeze, sorry.

ELLIE

> It's just not appropriate right now.

JAY

> I'm not trying to be appropriate.

ELLIE

> Dude.

JAY

> Can I pour us a drink please?

ELLIE

> Yeah yeah yeah.

Jay pours out two glasses from a decanter.

JAY

> Sweet baby Jesus this is good.

ELLIE

> Wait—you just got out of rehab . . .

JAY

> So what? It's not for me. Sobriety. 12 step meetings—all that confession and affectionate healing bullshit. I don't wanna heal. I want to suffer. It's more human . . .

ELLIE

> I'm *not* kissing you right now Jay. Come on.

JAY

> Now I'm a sad boi.

ELLIE

> Slow down.

JAY

> No.

ELLIE

> Jay—

JAY

> It's my alcohol!

ELLIE

    Fine. Be sloppy. Fuck it.

JAY

    Thank you!

ELLIE

    Don't be this person . . .

JAY

    It's impossible: the behavior is stronger than I am. I am the behavior.

ELLIE

    It's kind of fascinating . . .

JAY

    A part of me just like wishes there was some violence I could sign up for, some kind of war I could go to. There's no amount of cruelty I wouldn't inflict on my fellow humans if someone would just give me permission—

ELLIE

    Fascist.

JAY

    Sure. At least I'm not a bland little bitch like you.

ELLIE

    Thanks.

JAY

    You know, sometimes I honestly think I'm a woman, or would be happier as a woman.

ELLIE

    Oh wow Jay.

JAY

    I'm not joking around.

ELLIE

    I don't know how to receive that information—

JAY

    As the whiskey is telling you its secrets.

ELLIE

    I see.

JAY

    I mean, isn't your brother trans?

ELLIE

My sister now—

JAY

Right, same thing—

ELLIE

Uh no, not same thing; and that doesn't make me an expert on how to think about you or how anybody else should think about their body—

JAY

Ok—but I'm actually reaching out to you in this moment though—

ELLIE

Ok, you want my advice? Go chop off your dick—have a blast—you'll love having a gaping wound between your legs—

JAY

Whoa.

ELLIE

I just feel like you're doing everything possible to elicit a reaction from me—

JAY

So you think what I'm telling you is not sincere?

ELLIE

Not particularly.

JAY

What if it's a cry for help?

ELLIE

Then it's a cry for help directed at someone who can't help you.

JAY

Forget I said anything.

ELLIE

Will do.

JAY

Don't hate me.

ELLIE

Whatever is happening between them is going to fade away.

JAY

I wish I had that attitude, but it obsesses me.

ELLIE
Because your property is being trespassed on.

JAY
I don't see her as property—

ELLIE
No, you just treat her like it—

JAY
No ...

ELLIE
Great comeback.

JAY
So I take it you're prepared to play the good cop—

ELLIE
I said I would accompany you; I didn't say I would take your side completely.

JAY
Goddammit.

ELLIE
What exactly did you expect?

JAY
That you'd throw fuel on the fire.

ELLIE
I'm ready to take a more enlightened attitude.

JAY
I'm not.

ELLIE
I don't see how that's gonna make anything better.

JAY
Don't judge something you don't understand.

ELLIE
I could say the same thing about Liz and Nick.

JAY
They're bad people.

ELLIE
They're just people.

JAY

    No. They're bad. They enjoy the idea of causing other people pain.

ELLIE

    No they don't Jay.

JAY

    Can you just fucking say 'yes Jay, you're right Jay'—it would be therapeutic for me.

ELLIE

    We're here to get things out in the open, not put them on trial.

JAY

    Speak for yourself.

ELLIE

    If we're not on the same page, then I probably should go.

JAY

    No don't I'm scared.

ELLIE

    Ok, then you have to chill.

JAY

    I have no chill.

ELLIE

    Somehow I knew you were going to say that.

JAY

    I feel even more insecure that you've been able to take this all in stride relatively.

ELLIE

    If Nick is eaten up by guilt, all the better for me honestly.

JAY

    Damn.

ELLIE

    I don't need him to be in love with me; I could care less actually. That's not the point of a relationship to me, actually.

JAY

    What is then?

ELLIE

    The point of a relationship is to have one.

JAY

    Just to have one—

ELLIE
I'm happier wanting less—

JAY
I can't say the same—

ELLIE
Maybe you should—

JAY
Nor can I say that I get what you're about Ellie—

ELLIE
Dude--you have no interest in me as a human being whatsoever. There's really no point into going into details regarding beliefs, values, ideas. Like, none. You're not interested in anything that doesn't confirm what you already believe or strays too far from the topic of 'you'.

JAY
True.

ELLIE
There has to be some part of you that's aware of the part of you that speaks—there has to be.

JAY
Yes, and he's miserable. Absolutely miserable.

ELLIE
How old is he?

JAY
I would say he's about 12—that's when he got sliced off from the primary ego.

ELLIE
Fascinating.

JAY
I'm in wild amounts of emotional distress right now.

ELLIE
How fun for you.

JAY
I need some kind of order in my life Ellie.

ELLIE
All alcoholics do.

JAY

> You really do not like me one bit.

ELLIE

> I'm just not going to validate your narcissistic delusions.

JAY

> Her text messages to him are really fucking sad.

ELLIE

> I couldn't read them honestly—when you sent them—

JAY

> Sad sad sad.

ELLIE

> On some level, all of us just need to talk—like—from beginning to end. With complete honesty.

JAY

> Define complete—

ELLIE

> Like everyone takes responsibility for their side of things.

JAY

> Hell no.

ELLIE

> I'm trying to help you Jay.

JAY

> Liz and I have sex like once a month—or less—did you know that?

ELLIE

> Nick and I fuck all the time.

JAY

> Man, what is the secret? Like—how does he do it?

ELLIE

> His secret is that he's available.

JAY

> I'm available!

ELLIE

> No, but you're not Jay; you're not functional enough to be available. Nick is pure function.

JAY

And this is what you want in a partner?

ELLIE

I'm telling you: I have zero idealizations around the idea of a relationship. If someone wants to go through life with me, and like, keep the bad shit to a minimum, then I think I can love them for that.

JAY

Is he keeping bad shit to a minimum?

ELLIE

I honestly think he's trying.

JAY

You seem like a person in denial.

ELLIE

Call it what you will.

JAY

Why are you here?

ELLIE

To stop you from making too big a scene.

JAY

I'm so drunk.

ELLIE

Hey uh, I got a text from Nick.

JAY

What does it say?

ELLIE

He wants to meet up. He's obviously not with Elizabeth—

JAY

Really?

ELLIE

I think so?

JAY

Jesus Christ.

ELLIE

Yeah it's wild.

JAY

I guess they had a fight or something.

ELLIE

Is that a good thing in your mind?

JAY

I just want things to go back to normal. So. Yeah. Sure. It is.

ELLIE

So then we don't really disagree about this, do we?

JAY

The more I examine my life, the more pointless it seems. I'm a computer attached to a semen pump. It's ridiculous.

ELLIE

Does that make me an egg-sac guided by an algorithm?

JAY

Yes it does.

ELLIE

No wonder you're depressed, if that's how you see things.

JAY

Are you religious?

ELLIE

Spiritual.

JAY

So you go to yoga twice a week—?

ELLIE

Essentially.

JAY

Yeah see that's garbage.

ELLIE

It's better than nothing.

JAY

No, it is nothing.

ELLIE

Probably.

JAY

    I guess this really isn't happening then? All that build up.

ELLIE

    Honestly, who knows what's going on. I certainly don't.

JAY

    Welp.

ELLIE

    I'm gonna get going.

JAY

    See ya.

Ellie leaves. Blackout.

Four

Jay passed out on the couch, enter Elizabeth, looking upset.

ELIZABETH
Hey—

JAY
Hi—

ELIZABETH
You're home—

JAY
I am. You're also home—

ELIZABETH
No—but you're supposed to be in California—

JAY
Never got on the plane.

ELIZABETH
I see that.

JAY
Isn't it fun!

ELIZABETH
Have you been drinking?

JAY
What kind of question is that? Of course I've been drinking. What does it look like?

ELIZABETH
I guess it was a rhetorical question.

JAY
Shit in my mouth and call it cotton candy.

ELIZABETH
What?

JAY
Amen!

ELIZABETH
What?

JAY
> Can I get an amen?

JAY
> Amen! Can I get an Amen? Amen!

ELIZABETH
> Alright bud. Simmer down.

JAY
> Are you unhappy?

ELIZABETH
> Unhappy with what?

JAY
> Being married to me.

ELIZABETH
> What are you talking about? I'm perfectly happy—

JAY
> 'Perfectly'—

ELIZABETH
> Very?

JAY
> Mhm.

ELIZABETH
> What evidence have I given you to the contrary?

JAY
> Why aren't you pregnant yet?

ELIZABETH
> I'm not ready. You know that.

JAY
> I do?

ELIZABETH
> You don't remember our wedding night at all do you?

JAY
> Not after a certain point. Why?

ELIZABETH
> You told me things.

JAY

Like what?

ELIZABETH

Just things.

JAY

You're making me spiral.

ELIZABETH

I'm just trying to have a conversation, but I guess that's impossible.

JAY

Impossible's a good word.

ELIZABETH

Why?

JAY

All I have are negative thoughts.

ELIZABETH

Right Jay, whatever.

JAY

You've never seen me cry—

ELIZABETH

No I haven't.

JAY

How have you never asked me about that? Why aren't you ever, like—"dude, your emotions are coming out in all the wrong ways!"—?

ELIZABETH

Why are you bringing this up now?

JAY

I was dreaming of tears the way vegans dream of steak. . . . I haven't cried since I was ten I think.

ELIZABETH

What happened when you were ten?

JAY

I dunno. My turtle died or some shit. Whatever. I just remember weeping at dinner one night and my family just kinda staring at me, those frigid fucks.

ELIZABETH

Your mother is worried about you.

JAY
What, did she call you?

ELIZABETH
Yeah, we talk.

JAY
Why?! Why why why?!

ELIZABETH
She's my family now too.

JAY
I don't know why that fact does make you jump out the window honestly.

ELIZABETH
She's nice to me.

JAY
Just wait. She was nice to me too at first.

ELIZABETH
Actually, I'm starting to wonder if the stories you told me about her are even true—

JAY
Hello darkness my old friend.

ELIZABETH
Oh Jay . . .

JAY
My back really hurts; I think I fell asleep in a weird position. Can you give me a massage?

ELIZABETH
Must I?

JAY
I'd really appreciate it . . .

ELIZABETH
Alright alright.

Elizabeth begins to massage Jay.

JAY
Ah that feels good.

ELIZABETH
I'm glad.

JAY

You looked upset when you walked in just now.

ELIZABETH

I don't think you'd understand.

JAY

Why's that?

ELIZABETH

It's something very private.

JAY

Ok Liz.

ELIZABETH

I need to keep some things to myself; I'm sure you could say the same of yourself.

JAY

I guess I could. Oh—that's a tender spot—right there—dig that out baby—

ELIZABETH

You're really tense.

JAY

Oof that kinda hurts actually. On second thought.

ELIZABETH

Get over it.

JAY

Yes Daddy.

ELIZABETH	JAY
You know it kinda pisses me off to come home to find you not only not where you said you would be, but completely wasted. Like, I had to listen to you praise the wonders of sobriety for six months and have my own drinking policed. And now you're all about booze again, like you never stopped.	Dear Diary. The sadness fills you up. Your belly bloats. You feel listless and you don't mind what people say. Money is wasted, care is wasted. Something strange happens where the mind disorders itself for the sake of producing a new kind of content to feed on; it's really an odd sensation.

ELIZABETH

You're off in your own world . . . You're just tuning out as always. Ignoring what's in front of you.

JAY

    Totally.

ELIZABETH

    Jay: it just takes a toll living with bipolar.

JAY

    Sorry.

ELIZABETH

    I might as well mark the calendar for ups and downs and super-downs and super-ups. . . .

JAY

    I said sorry—

ELIZABETH

    Anticipating your moods has kind of re-wired my entire nervous system –

JAY

    I accept that. Do you still love me though?

ELIZABETH

    Sure Jay, I love you.

JAY

    Well that's good at least.

ELIZABETH

    Yeah it's fantastic.

JAY

    Ah! That's the spot! Right there!

Blackout . . .

Five

The quartet: back together for a drink.

JAY

    You guys still have the post-honeymoon glow.

ELLIE

    I think that has more to do with me quitting my job.

NICK

    It's wearing off fast, I promise.

JAY

    You quit?

ELLIE

    Totally.

JAY

    I thought you were into it.

ELLIE

    It was pretty draining and evil, so.

ELIZABETH

    So what's the plan?

ELLIE

    Oh God. Um. Just not work for awhile. Maybe start a business or something. But, I'm not really in a rush.

NICK

    I'm making bank motherfucker. Corporate law was a good choice.

ELIZABETH

    Nick literally never fails to talk about money when we get together.

NICK

    Whoops.

JAY

    It's weird to be the sober one.

ELLIE

    You look so much healthier Jay—

JAY

    I'm trying.

ELIZABETH
>He really is.

JAY
>On the other hand, I'm also so bored that I want to go skydiving without a parachute—

ELIZABETH
>Wow, this is off to a great start . . .

NICK
>I'm actually glad to see you guys! Seriously!

JAY
>I heard you ran into Jon on the street.

NICK
>Yeah—fuck him.

JAY
>You didn't say hi? It's been a year.

NICK
>Did you talk to him? Did he say something?

JAY
>Yeah, he texted me.

NICK
>What'd he say?

JAY
>Just that you blew him off.

NICK
>That's it?

JAY
>Yeah.

NICK
>He didn't say he's sorry for—

JAY
>Don't be so butt-hurt.

NICK
>People are so weird. Like, he was the aggressor; but then he wants my brotherly affection? Fuck that.

JAY
>Don't shoot the messenger . . .

NICK

Fair enough.

ELIZABETH

Personally, I feel completely ready to move on from my younger self and a vast majority of my old social connections. Just doesn't seem productive or interesting to dwell.

ELLIE

I feel that.

ELIZABETH

But perhaps the boys don't want to let go of their glory days—

NICK

I've let go; it's just . . .

ELLIE

It's just what?

NICK

I feel like there's something weak about forgiving betrayals as if nothing happened. . . . What?

ELLIE

I'll tell you later.

JAY

Annnnnddddd tonight is actually going to kick me off the wagon. Hard.

ELLIE

We're just being us.

JAY

Can't argue with that.

ELIZABETH

I guess the four of us are just . . . pretty passionate people . . . in our own way.

NICK

Uh. Sure.

ELIZABETH

You don't agree Nick?

NICK

Who knows honestly.

JAY

All I have are negative thoughts.

ELIZABETH
That's been his catchphrase for the last year.

JAY
D'ya'll like it?

ELLIE
Love it Jay.

JAY
Thank you, thank you.

NICK
I guess tonight is going to be a strictly lights-up affair, huh?

ELLIE
Absolutely.

ELIZABETH
Was it even a question?

NICK
A 'fuck reunion' would be interesting . . .

ELLIE
No it wouldn't.

NICK
Come on! It would be so interesting—

JAY
Dude, I don't want to be interesting anymore. I'm anti-interesting.

NICK
Too bad.

JAY
Refusal, impotence, passivity: this is how I roll.

ELLIE
Cute.

NICK
Am I the only one who thinks we owe it to ourselves to try?

ELLIE
What exactly do we owe Nick?

NICK
I dunno how to articulate it, but—

ELLIE

But what? I'm curious—

NICK

I'm asking, like, do we really want to get stuck?

ELLIE

Whatdya mean?

NICK

Normal. Do we want to just be normal people?

JAY

Absolutely.

ELIZABETH

I can't take this anymore . . .

JAY

Take what?

ELIZABETH

Never mind. I just need a drink.

NICK

What's wrong Liz?

ELIZABETH

I want to tell Ellie something that Jay told me while blacked out on our wedding night—

JAY

Abort, abort!

ELIZABETH

Ellie—did Nick ever tell you how he and Jay used to get drunk . . . and fuck after frat parties?

ELLIE

No. He didn't. Are you joking?

ELIZABETH

No—I can't say I am.

ELLIE

Gotcha.

NICK

What do you want me to say?

ELLIE

I don't want you to say anything Nick.

NICK
    Alright.

ELLIE
    Life's just so funny.

NICK
    Yeah it's hilarious—a real hoot.

JAY
    Tears! Real ones!

ELIZABETH
    You know, maybe we should just see what happens tonight.

ELLIE
    Yeah. Maybe.

NICK
    I wouldn't mind.

JAY
    Ok . . . I need a drink.

ELIZABETH
    Of course you do.

NICK
    Let me pick the music.

JAY
    Son of a fucking bitch.

                    ELIZABETH   ELLIE
    Jay . . .   Nothing pretentious please—

NICK
    Relax. It's gonna be great.

Berlin Story

"I'm the sort of woman who can take men away from their wives, but I could never keep anybody for long. And that's because I'm the type which every man imagines he wants, until he gets me; and then he finds he doesn't really, after all."

—Christopher Isherwood, *Goodbye to Berlin*

Berlin Story premiered at Matt & Cassidy's loft in Greenpoint, Brooklyn in July of 2022 with the following cast:

Maeve: Cassidy Grady
Frank: Christian Lorentzen
Monika: Anni Baumann
Adam: David Levine
Clem: Nancy Hine

Directed by Matthew Gasda
Assistant Direction by Sarah De Baets

Cast of Characters

Frank: 45, a pornographer abroad
Maeve: 24, ex-cam girl
Monika: Mid-20s German, lively
Clem: 25 ish, gallery girl, British
Adam: anywhere between 30–50, war reporter

Setting

Frank and Maeve, Frank's Berlin flat, which he shares with Adam. Very cool place; pictures of pinups on the walls and sexy art books on the coffee-table. Glossy magazines. Vinyls. Paperback novels.

One

MAEVE
> You're not saying much.

FRANK
> I have to maintain my air of knowingness.

MAEVE
> Yeah, but it's me.

FRANK
> Do you want a beer?

MAEVE
> Sure.

FRANK
> Dope.

MAEVE
> I feel like I'm imposing.

FRANK
> You're fine.

MAEVE
> You're being polite . . .

FRANK
> I'm just on the ropes with this chick—

MAEVE
> The one you were telling me about?

FRANK
> Yeah.

MAEVE
> She's my age?

FRANK
> A little older.

MAEVE
> How'd you meet her? Is she industry?

FRANK
> No—uh. Just at a bar. She lives in London, but she works for an art gallery and they have a branch in Berlin.

MAEVE
> Does she want to move here?

FRANK
> Sore subject.

MAEVE
> Sorry.

FRANK
> But yeah, it would be better if she just lived here.

MAEVE
> This flat or Berlin?

FRANK
> Yes.

MAEVE
> Aw, are you getting domestic Frank?

FRANK
> I've always been domestic; I'm the lovechild of Hugh Hefner and Martha Stewart.

Maeve browses the bookshelf. Maeve takes out a copy of Schopenhauer.

MAEVE
> Is this book yours, could I borrow it?

FRANK
> It's my roommate's, but I don't think he'd care.

MAEVE
> What's his name again?

FRANK
> Adam. We go way back.

MAEVE
> What does he do?

FRANK
> He's a journalist—

MAEVE
> Cute—

FRANK
> Like a war correspondent.

MAEVE
Cute—

FRANK
So he has a death wish.

MAEVE
Cute—

FRANK
Yeah, he's a cool guy.

MAEVE
There's good energy in this flat. I like it.

FRANK
It's, uh, carefully cultivated.

MAEVE
Are you happy here?

FRANK
Ecstatic.

MAEVE
You don't miss New York at all?

FRANK
Not really.

MAEVE
I'm personally kind of over it as well; I'd move here, but I don't even know what I'd do.

FRANK
You don't have to do anything; that's the whole point of Berlin.

MAEVE
If you say so.

FRANK
What have you been doing for money in New York?

MAEVE
I have a sugar daddy, but the thing is—I don't even have to fuck him. Just like go out to dinner a few times a month. But I'd have to find someone else or something if I moved here—

FRANK
It's not hard.

MAEVE

Yeah but mentally it's a hurdle—

FRANK

Sure.

MAEVE

What Frank? I really don't wanna start doing porn again.

FRANK

I'm not saying you should.

MAEVE

Then what are you saying?

FRANK

I'm saying just do what you want, don't overthink it.

MAEVE

Right now what I want is to feel safe and secure to be completely honest.

FRANK

Cool.

MAEVE

You're making me nervous.

FRANK

Whoops.

MAEVE

Just tell me to fuck off if you don't want me to be here.

FRANK

Maeve you're my friend; it's fine; you can stay here; I already told you.

MAEVE

But a part of you hates it—

FRANK

Yeah, so?

MAEVE

I don't like taking advantage of your honor code.

FRANK

That's what honor codes are for.

MAEVE

If your lover shows up, I'll disappear; you don't have to worry.

FRANK
>Whatever it's fine.

MAEVE
>Can I be honest?

FRANK
>Give it a shot.

MAEVE
>I think the real reason that you sense that I'm actually here out of pity for you—

FRANK
>Drink your beer.

FRANK
>How long are you going to be in Europe?

MAEVE
>Three weeks. He's meeting me here on Sunday, then we're going to Basel, Milan, Paris . . . the south of France . . .

FRANK
>The grand tour.

MAEVE
>I feel really stupid.

FRANK
>Don't.

MAEVE
>Can we listen to some music?

FRANK
>Yeah.

MAEVE
>I think I need to find someone to hook up with tonight.

FRANK
>Go for it—just not here.

MAEVE
>I know—

FRANK
>Cool—

MAEVE
>I think . . .

FRANK

Maeve . . .

MAEVE

My impulse control is a little wonky sometimes, sorry.

FRANK

I don't want to walk in on you getting doubled by two guys both named Hans. I don't feel like working this weekend; you know what I mean?

MAEVE

Don't worry. I heard you're doing more like art stuff; like photography.

FRANK

Yeah, I'm in this exhibition next month.

MAEVE

Fuck, I'm gonna miss it; I'm sad.

FRANK

It's fine.

MAEVE

Frank—

FRANK

Sup?

MAEVE

Why does my brain do this?

FRANK

Do what?

MAEVE

Origami with situations.

FRANK

No idea.

MAEVE

The number of panic attacks that I have but I don't tell people about is astronomical.

FRANK

Are you having a panic attack?

MAEVE

I never really know in the moment.

FRANK

I guess I'll just have to find out.

MAEVE

It was actually fun working with you, you know—

FRANK

As opposed to—

MAEVE

Manipulators and monsters.

FRANK

Nice to know I'm not one of those.

MAEVE

No, you're actually great.

FRANK

Thanks. I don't get a lot of compliments these days.

MAEVE

You make me sad.

FRANK

Sorry.

MAEVE

It's not your fault, but you just do.

FRANK

I should be more conscious of my bad vibes. Whoops.

MAEVE

Do you love her?

FRANK

The chick?

MAEVE

Yeah.

FRANK

Love is a word, sure.

MAEVE

But like really—?

FRANK

A little, yeah.

MAEVE

Have you told her?

FRANK
    She gets it.

MAEVE
    Does she?

FRANK
    Yeah. She's on the level.

MAEVE
    I think you should tell her.

FRANK
    I'd prefer not to.

MAEVE
    Why?

FRANK
    Because I prefer not to.

MAEVE
    You shouldn't be afraid of pain.

FRANK
    Profound.

MAEVE
    Well.

FRANK
    Yeah.

MAEVE
    I really just want to *lure* someone in tonight.

FRANK
    You have options.

MAEVE
    I know.

FRANK
    Do you?

MAEVE
    Kinda. Am I being insecure?

FRANK

A little.

MAEVE

That's how I'm feeling I guess.

FRANK

It happens.

MAEVE

Or maybe I just feign insecurity to get people to respond to me a certain way. Can never tell.

MAEVE

Why have I never lured you?

FRANK

Have you ever tried?

MAEVE

All the time.

FRANK

I don't think that's true.

MAEVE

We can pretend.

FRANK

I guess.

MAEVE

Do you feel bad for yourself?

FRANK

It depends.

MAEVE

On what?

FRANK

What time the bar opens.

MAEVE

I see.

FRANK

You can join me if you want.

MAEVE

I'll come for a little bit, but I kinda wanna do my own thing eventually.

FRANK
>That's cool.

MAEVE
>Are you annoyed at me?

FRANK
>No.

MAEVE
>You seem annoyed.

FRANK
>Nah.

MAEVE
>Ok but.

FRANK
>What?

MAEVE
>I just wanna feel like you're glad to see me.

FRANK
>You're a ray of sunshine kid. Happy?

MAEVE
>We used to have such amazing talks.

FRANK
>We can have another one sometime.

MAEVE
>What about right now?

FRANK
>If this conversation was meant to be 'amazing'—it would be by now. I see you've curled up in the fetal position.

MAEVE
>Yeah. I have.

FRANK
>Alright then.

MAEVE
>I feel like I have been avoiding my issues for so long that I've begun to think of them as strengths.

FRANK
Good luck with that.

MAEVE
Can you slap me across the face?

FRANK
No.

MAEVE
Too bad.

FRANK
Not my thing.

MAEVE
Being gentle with a woman is a sign of disrespect.

FRANK
I don't agree.

MAEVE
There's an industry party tomorrow night if you wanna go.

FRANK
Maybe.

MAEVE
It might be fun.

FRANK
I'm post-fun.

MAEVE
Yeah you're old.

FRANK
I guess.

MAEVE
You just need to find the right person.

FRANK
That sounds lame.

MAEVE
I want you to be happy.

FRANK
I wanna go to the bar.

MAEVE

Right now?

FRANK

I believe my local opened two minutes ago.

MAEVE

Frank.

FRANK

What Maeve?

MAEVE

It's alright that you're feeling lonesome, but it would be nice if you stopped taking it out on me.

FRANK

Sure thing.

MAEVE

I think I did something really stupid today.

FRANK

What's that?

MAEVE

I broke up with someone I really really really really love before I got on the plane this morning.

FRANK

Yeah that seems pretty stupid.

MAEVE

It was.

FRANK

Just call him.

MAEVE

No, no. I can't.

FRANK

Why not.

MAEVE

Because the way I did it, the way I said it, was really really bad and now it's very very final.

FRANK

Sucks.

MAEVE
Yeah it sucks a lot.

FRANK
Sorry about that.

MAEVE
In my relationships I tend to vacillate wildly between emotionally needy and emotionally cold. I'm begging for closeness in one moment, and then in the next I'm just treating the person like the lowest of the low—

FRANK
Yeah, you probably should stop doing that.

MAEVE
I'm trying.

FRANK
One thing I've learned is that chaos in people is a sign that they're trying to preserve their independence in some way; it's a way of keeping other people from getting too close.

MAEVE
I'm just more comfortable this way I think.

FRANK
What way?

MAEVE
Just doing my thing.

FRANK
That's cool.

MAEVE
It's tragic.

FRANK
It can be both.

MAEVE
I think I fall in love with ideas and into despair with real things . . . which I think is my way of remaining attached to childhood, or like, a child, in a way, despite my entrance into like literally the 'adult' world. Like, I think often my rage and despair is just resistance to the thought that things will never be truly magical—

FRANK
The trick is giving up certain illusions without becoming cynical.

MAEVE

You're so cynical.

FRANK

Not at all.

MAEVE

You come off that way.

FRANK

I'm shielding my higher truths with irony obviously.

MAEVE

Yeah, but.

FRANK

But what?

MAEVE

I'm confused.

FRANK

Don't be.

MAEVE

Ok . . . Frank?

FRANK

Yes Maeve—

MAEVE

Am I wasting my life?

FRANK

I have no idea.

MAEVE

Because I feel like I am.

FRANK

Why's that?

MAEVE

There are moments when I see that my self-esteem is getting bound up with the most kind of like facile and materialistic bullshit; like I crave attention from people I don't respect and I get so high on their fake affection when they come to my parties and shit, like—

FRANK

When you're young, it's easy to confuse flattery for love and love for flattery.

MAEVE
> What do I do then?

FRANK
> Keep mortality in mind.

MAEVE
> Scary.

FRANK
> Yeah.

MAEVE
> Anyway—let's just go; can we go? I need a drink.

FRANK
> Alright.

MAEVE
> Can we just sit here for a moment actually?

FRANK
> Goddammit.

MAEVE
> Sorry. Anxiety. Fuck.

FRANK
> Take your time.

MAEVE
> Would you want to be my father in a spiritual sense?

FRANK
> No.

MAEVE
> Ok. That's sad and disappointing.

FRANK
> Sorry.

MAEVE
> I just feel like I need a spiritual father very badly.

FRANK
> Have you tried God?

MAEVE
> I don't think He's available.

FRANK

I'd try again later if he doesn't pick up. Or leave a voice mail.

MAEVE

You're one of the good ones Frank; I want you to know.

FRANK

Thanks. You ready to go?

MAEVE

Yeah I am.

They leave.

Two

Enter Adam and Monika, his German lover.

Adam notices the Schopenhauer on the table.

MONIKA
> I don't know why you had to say that.

ADAM
> Neither do I, but I did.

A pause.

MONIKA
> What?

ADAM
> Nothing.

MONIKA
> What a little bitch boy.

ADAM
> Sorry.

MONIKA
> I mean, you are—

ADAM
> I'm not denying it.

MONIKA
> You hide.

ADAM
> Hide where?

MONIKA
> Everywhere. You're always hiding.

ADAM
> Expert analysis.

MONIKA
> And you run. You run and hide. You're either hiding and running.

ADAM

    I'm right here Monika, relax.

MONIKA

    Why don't you live alone? You're too old to live with someone.

ADAM

    I like it.

MONIKA

    Can I have a drink?

ADAM

    Yeah go crazy.

MONIKA

    What do you have?

ADAM

    Whatever's on the table.

MONIKA

    You live like animals.

ADAM

    Should we go to a hotel?

MONIKA

    Why haven't you learned any German?

ADAM

    Ich weiß nicht.

MONIKA

    Bitch. Boy.

ADAM

    Monika . . .

MONIKA

    Do you think I have a nice ass?

ADAM

    It's not bad.

MONIKA

    Do you think I have a nice pussy? A nice, *tight, wet* pussy?

ADAM

    Sure.

MONIKA

Do you want me?

ADAM

For the most part.

MONIKA

Wrong answer. *Do you want me?*

ADAM

I want a lot of things.

MONIKA

Look at me—

ADAM

But the window's so interesting.

MONIKA

Please?

ADAM

I really don't feel like it.

MONIKA

You *ass*.

ADAM

Speaking of—can I fuck your ass tonight?

MONIKA

No. Maybe.

ADAM

We'll circle back.

MONIKA

I thought you were passionate, not just depraved.

ADAM

It's easy to confuse the two things.

MONIKA

Yes it is.

ADAM

Does your husband know you're with me?

MONIKA

Of course he does. Also, I'm free. It doesn't matter. Who cares?

ADAM

I've never seen an open relationship work.

MONIKA

You're actually remarkably incurious for someone whose job it is to notice things.

ADAM

I don't cover first world problems, you know?

MONIKA

Bravo.

ADAM

Bend over.

MONIKA

Why?

ADAM

I wanna give you a spank.

MONIKA

Ok . . .

ADAM

You deserve it.

MONIKA

I've been naughty, haven't I Daddy?

ADAM

So naughty.

MONIKA

Well. I'm waiting—

ADAM

I've gone limp, my apologies.

MONIKA

Tease.

ADAM

What is your father like?

MONIKA

He's an architect.

ADAM

Was he ever sexual with you as a child?

230 • Berlin Story

MONIKA

I remember that I would shower with him when I was very little; I suppose that was a little strange. But that was about it. . . . Weird question.

ADAM

Actually, it should be a standard question. Like, job interview: "Did anyone in your family ever rape you?" I feel like the world would be so much less chaotic if people just got that out of the way first.

MONIKA

Ok—did anyone ever rape you?

ADAM

I *wish*, but no. Next question.

MONIKA

Are you in love with anyone?

ADAM

Do you want my answer to be you?

MONIKA

I know you're not in love with me, that's why I'm asking.

ADAM

I am. Yeah.

MONIKA

Who?

ADAM

That's my business.

MONIKA

Who?

ADAM

Lay off.

MONIKA

Why do you make me so angry?

ADAM

Are you in love with me?

MONIKA

A little bit unfortunately.

ADAM

I feel like you would have made an amazing Nazi. You were born too late my friend.

MONIKA

I don't think I want to sleep with you tonight.

ADAM

No worries.

MONIKA

I thought I did, but I changed my mind.

ADAM

Is there some kind of way to repair this interaction?

MONIKA

There might be, but I'm not sure if you're willing to really be sincere with me and try.

ADAM

Why does repairing require sincerity?

MONIKA

Because trust requires sincerity.

ADAM

Does it?

MONIKA

Almost certainly. Would you like to meet my husband?

ADAM

Not really. Does he want to meet me?

MONIKA

Yeah. He read your book.

ADAM

You gave him my book?

MONIKA

No, he read it on his own.

ADAM

In German or English?

MONIKA

He read the translation.

ADAM

Is it good?

MONIKA

I guess, yeah. Don't be so insecure.

ADAM

> Impossible.

MONIKA

> How much longer are you in town?

ADAM

> I'm leaving for assignment tomorrow.

MONIKA

> I feel like we should try to start fresh when you get back.

ADAM

> Once things start to rot, there's no way to turn them fresh again in my humble opinion. But sure, we can try.

MONIKA

> You're afraid that you might actually have feelings for me—

> *Adam leafs through the copy of Schopenhauer that Maeve left on the table.*

ADAM

> "Life swings like a pendulum backward and forward between pain and boredom."

MONIKA

> Where are you going on assignment?

ADAM

> I'm not telling.

MONIKA

> Why not?

ADAM

> There's supreme, supreme pleasure in getting on a plane and just not having to explain yourself or justify yourself or maintain your little bourgeoisie world.

MONIKA

> What's the closest you've ever come to dying?

ADAM

> Probably last year in Karachi.

MONIKA

> Doing what?

ADAM

> You know, there was a situation.

MONIKA

Adam—

ADAM

That's me—

MONIKA

If I fuck you tonight, I'll never see you again. But if I don't fuck you tonight, I'm open to see you as much as you want.

ADAM

I'd rather fuck.

MONIKA

It's ridiculous that I have feelings for you of any kind.

ADAM

When your father would shower with you, would he lather your body, or would you wash yourself?

MONIKA

We should fuck just so you shut up.

ADAM

Sounds like a fun idea.

MONIKA

I wanted you to say you want to see me again though.

ADAM

What if I don't *though*?

MONIKA

I'd be extremely hurt.

ADAM

Good.

MONIKA

Is that really what you want? To hurt me?

ADAM

Yes.

MONIKA

You were so romantic and charming when we met.

ADAM

Yeah—last month was, like, a different lifetime honestly.

MONIKA
Do you always turn on people?

ADAM
More or less.

MONIKA
At least I'm not the only one.

ADAM
You're part of a proud and noble tradition.

MONIKA
My husband is with someone else tonight too.

ADAM
What's she like?

MONIKA
Oh I have no idea. Knowing him, he probably just went to a bar and picked someone up.

ADAM
As revenge on you for being with me?

MONIKA
For revenge, and just for pleasure, if there's a difference.

ADAM
There's no difference.

MONIKA
Ah.

ADAM
It doesn't sound like either of you want to be married, if you ask me.

MONIKA
You really lack all subtlety—like, mentally.

ADAM
Probably, yeah.

MONIKA
Sorry but it's true.

ADAM
He's a lot older than you right?

MONIKA
Like ten years.

ADAM
What does he do?

MONIKA
I've told you this multiple times before.

He's an artist—

a painter—

ADAM

We get wasted every time we're together.

Berlin—

right?—

ADAM
Is he good?

MONIKA
He's successful.

ADAM
But is he talented?

MONIKA
I think so.

ADAM
That's a no.

MONIKA
He's very talented.

ADAM
Stop pretending, you cunt. He's trash. He's a fraud.

MONIKA
I'm invested in you for all the wrong reasons aren't I?

ADAM
Probably.

MONIKA
I find your loneliness very attractive.

ADAM
I'm not lonely; I'm indifferent; let's be clear.

MONIKA
You're intensely lonely; you can't fool me. Do you want to put on some music?

ADAM
I'm not in the mood.

MONIKA

I'm trying to change the mood. I wanna wiggle.

ADAM

I don't wiggle.

MONIKA

I wanna feel things.

ADAM

Tragic.

MONIKA

I mean, just spare me the pose; I'm so over it.

ADAM

What pose?

MONIKA

Oh you have so many poses, or so many variations on the same pose; I lose track.

ADAM

Right.

MONIKA

When I met you—you wanna know what I thought? I thought: I wish I knew him before he turned into *this* person—

ADAM

I've always been *this* person.

MONIKA

I don't believe that, not actually.

ADAM

Because you choose not to.

MONIKA

Why is it so hard for you to believe that I want a fulfilling connection with you?

ADAM

I don't get all this poly bullshit; I'm sorry. *I don't want a love experience.* I don't even know what that would entail.

MONIKA

Can you just be nice?

ADAM

This is my way of being nice.

MONIKA

    That's completely insane.

ADAM

    That's completely honest.

MONIKA

    You really think of yourself as an honest person, don't you?

ADAM

    Well. That's a complicated question.

MONIKA	ADAM
You act this way because you don't think anyone could actually care for you—	Plenty of people care for me;
	that's nice for them
Just respond	
	but
please	
	it just doesn't do much for me.
to what I said—	
MONIKA	**ADAM**
Adam, I think	
	Wow.
you truly despise yourself—	
	Yeah.
I can see it in your eyes.	
	The beautiful thing about forcing you to speak a second language is that you can never say anything . . .
What a jerk . . .	
	insightful.

Pause.

MONIKA

    I'm not your adversary. I'm not competing with you for anything. Do you understand that?

ADAM

    That is not my understanding actually.

MONIKA

    How do you see things, then, Adam?

ADAM

>What I see is that the reality principle and the pleasure principle have gotten badly confused here—

MONIKA

>Ok. Uh?

ADAM

>Yeah?

MONIKA

>I don't know. I don't know what to say. Tonight just took this dark turn. It started at dinner. You started being so awful. I don't understand it, but I'm trying to and you're not helping; you just keep deflecting and mocking and mocking—

ADAM

>You say things that annoy me. You annoy me.

MONIKA

>I think it annoys you that I'm more interested in *you* than what you *do*.

ADAM

>True.

MONIKA

>You wanna buy people drinks and have them ask you questions about everything you've seen; I've seen you do it—*you love it.* . . . It might be the only thing you like: being the center of attention.

ADAM

>Absolutely.

MONIKA

>It's sort of unbelievable that you can be this *old* and have this little self-awareness.

ADAM

>Monika, you're so painfully stupid. It would be merciful if we could just stop talking.

MONIKA

>There is something deeply wrong with you.

ADAM

>This should not come as news to anyone.

MONIKA

>I don't know what's stopping you from simply being different.

ADAM

>I'm begging you to employ even the slightest amount of irony in your discourse with me.

MONIKA

Does it bother you that I say what's on my mind?

ADAM

Yes, it does.

MONIKA

I can stop in that case . . .

ADAM

Now you're going to drag your emotional injury around my flat like a wounded deer.

MONIKA

I'm finishing off the whiskey.

ADAM

I see that.

MONIKA

I want to melt into something.

ADAM

There's a whole big city out there.

MONIKA

But I want you.

ADAM

That's so embarrassing.

MONIKA

I know.

ADAM

The only explanation for your behavior is that you get off on debasing yourself for someone.

MONIKA

Growing up, I was in love with my best friend, whose name was Hannah. We took dance class together and I would watch the sweat begin to form on her collarbone at the beginning of every class and the only thing I could think to do was lick it off, though of course I never did. She went through puberty first and I think she is to this day the most beautiful woman I've ever met. I was just obsessed with her—obsessed— for years. I suffered incredibly. Finally, when I confessed my love to her, when we were about 16, she cut me off immediately and refused to speak to me.

ADAM

And then what?

MONIKA

Heart broken by Hannah, in order to console myself . . . I seduced the pastor's son from my church . . . and tried to convince him to run away with me.

ADAM

He didn't—

MONIKA

No.

ADAM

Why?

MONIKA

He was a good boy.

ADAM

So you got married so you'd have security while you pursued unattainable objects.

MONIKA

I'm much more attractive than you.

ADAM

Indisputably.

MONIKA

But that doesn't seem to faze you.

ADAM

I know what I'm worth.

MONIKA

You know what? Let's just please fuck and never speak again. Any way you want, you can have me.

ADAM

Perfect. Are you joking?

MONIKA

No. I'm not.

She kisses him.

Lights.

Three

Afternoon.

Frank and his on again/off again girlfriend Clem are hanging out.

CLEM
Are you good at chess?

FRANK
Pretty good, yeah.

CLEM
Will you play me?

FRANK
Later.

CLEM
Are you afraid I'll win?

FRANK
Not particularly, no.

CLEM
You're very cute.

FRANK
Am I?

CLEM
Yes.

FRANK
That's not normally how people describe me.

CLEM
It's how I'm describing you.

FRANK
Yes, but why?

CLEM
Because you are.

FRANK
You're being suspiciously friendly.

CLEM

    I am?

FRANK

    Everyone who's ever broken up with me has gotten really nice before pulling the plug.

CLEM

    I think it's important we establish a solid friendship. . . . It's always that other thing, you know?

FRANK

    Sure—but who doesn't like the 'other thing'—?

CLEM

    Sometimes it's nice to just be buds though.

FRANK

    Is it?

CLEM

    Very much so.

FRANK

    How was your flight?

CLEM

    A few babies almost threw up on me, but basically ok.

FRANK

    I hope you're planning to stay for more than a few days.

CLEM

    I have to be back in London by Thursday.

FRANK

    That's stupid.

CLEM

    Very stupid, but just how things go.

FRANK

    Do you tell people you have a boyfriend?

CLEM

    Why would I tell some chap in London that I'm seeing some geezer in Berlin once a month?

FRANK

    Because it's true.

CLEM
Are we seeing each other Frank?

FRANK
Yes. Perhaps too clearly.

CLEM
I find you very fascinating.

FRANK
That's reassuring.

CLEM
Can I spend a day on set with you sometime?

FRANK
If you want.

CLEM
Do you ever do gay stuff or is it all basically hetero?

FRANK
No. Gay stuff is a completely difference scene.

CLEM
Have you ever fucked the girl who's staying with you?

FRANK
No.

CLEM
Why not?

FRANK
She just doesn't need that kind of attention from me.

CLEM
Do you have a type Frank?

FRANK
Yeah, it's called: someone who can tolerate me.

CLEM
That must limit your options. Do you have any coffee?

FRANK
I can make you some.

CLEM
No that's alright.

FRANK
>No, it's fine. Takes two minutes.

Frank starts to make coffee, but continues the conversation from the kitchen area.

CLEM
>Why are we like this?

FRANK
>Like what?

CLEM
>Like *this*.

FRANK
>Beats me.

CLEM
>We're an odd match.

FRANK
>But a match nonetheless. How do you want your coffee?

CLEM
>Black is fine unless you have some oat milk.

FRANK
>I will never have any oat milk.

CLEM
>Ok so just black then.

FRANK
>What were you thinking about?

CLEM
>When?

FRANK
>Just now.

CLEM
>Things about things about people.

FRANK
>Which things, which people?

CLEM
>This man I sat next to at the airport this morning who told me he was going to visit his dying brother in Germany.

FRANK

A Kraut?

CLEM

No, English; his brother's wife is German and they haven't spoken for a decade because of some family squabble, but the brother's got cancer so he feels compelled to greet him on his deathbed.

FRANK

Yeah, so . . . I don't particularly enjoy the topics of 'cancer' and 'death.'

CLEM

Sorry.

FRANK

I'd rather talk about life.

CLEM

So let's talk about life then.

FRANK

What about it?

CLEM

Anything. I like how your mind works.

FRANK

How's that? How does it work?

CLEM

In little circles, like ripples on a pond.

FRANK

Poetic.

CLEM

You said you wanted to talk about life—so here's your chance, that's all I'm saying.

FRANK

When I think about life, I think about your beauty.

CLEM

That's sweet.

FRANK

Yeah, I'm sweet.

CLEM

What are you feeling right now?

FRANK

I don't talk about feelings; you just have to assume they're there.

CLEM

I think there's something slightly narcissistic about wanting people to be in a state of constantly wondering what you're thinking.

FRANK

So?

CLEM

I'm not going to play that game.

FRANK

I don't find what you're saying interesting, sorry.

CLEM

Do you really think I'm beautiful?

FRANK

Yes, correct.

CLEM

That's generous.

CLEM

It's interesting Frank: charisma seems to come with the territory of being you.

FRANK

Are you envious of that?

CLEM

Slightly, yes.

FRANK

I can tell.

CLEM

Oh really?

FRANK

The careerist in you can only see other people as competition, even when they aren't.

CLEM

I'll have to think about that one.

FRANK

Please do.

CLEM

You seem to be of two minds about me.

FRANK

And two hearts and one cock.

CLEM

I've enjoyed learning from you; I think, in a way, I'm addicted to it.

FRANK

And what is that exactly? What are you learning?

CLEM

I don't know how to explain it.

FRANK

Try to know.

CLEM

It has something to do with the way your eye and mind frame the world, the way you see; I see you seeing and that helps me see.

FRANK

How do you think I see things?

CLEM

Mournfully, and yet with great respect for particularities—for concreteness.

FRANK

Sounds pretentious.

CLEM

I really have no idea why you do what you do and not something else, but I've learned to accept that as one of your great mysteries.

FRANK

Maybe I just like it and am good at it and maybe it pays the bills.

CLEM

Well, I think there must be more to it.

FRANK

There is, but that's my business.

CLEM

Of course.

FRANK

But you want me to make it your business too.

CLEM

I'd be flattered if you did.

FRANK
Sorry, but no.

CLEM
I might stay at a hotel tonight Frank.

FRANK
Why would you do that?

CLEM
I have this gallery event tomorrow and I want to be well rested.

FRANK
That sounds like total bullshit.

CLEM
I want to be your friend.

FRANK
What—like we can't sleep together anymore?

CLEM
I think we can do like a last hurrah—but generally yes.

FRANK
Lame. Are you dating a chap back in London? Is that what's up?

CLEM
It's not important.

FRANK
Look, you can do whatever you want—but—

CLEM
But what?

FRANK
Never mind . . .

CLEM
What do you expect from me Frank—?—wait don't answer that question—

FRANK
Ok.

CLEM
I've never wanted you to expect anything from me; I can't offer you anything.

FRANK
I disagree.

CLEM

You're not hearing me.

FRANK

No, I'm just not sticking to the script you've written for this encounter.

CLEM

Yeah, and it's making things difficult

FRANK

Everything in your life has been planned out in advance, including this fling clearly—

CLEM

Oh yeah?

FRANK

You see an affair with an older, more accomplished man as part of your sentimental education; it's completely programmatic.

CLEM

Are you accomplished Frank?

FRANK

I'm a real goddamn artist.

CLEM	FRANK
I don't see any evidence of that actually—	Right,
What I see is someone who has systematically destroyed their abilities out of fear	because you're a representative of so-called real art—
	and give me a fucking break—
and self-loathing—	I'm not interested in that garbage

CLEM

You really hold me in contempt, don't you?

FRANK

Contempt isn't exactly the right word.

CLEM

This just isn't working for me Frank.

FRANK

You're taking *this* too lightly I think.

CLEM
I uh—I just feel like I need someone to grow with and you're fully formed already.

FRANK
I was fully formed by the time
I was your age.

Growth is a myth you've been sold.

The reality is self-preservation
against deterioration and
bourgeois assimilation.

CLEM
That's not an excuse to talk down
to me—

or patronize me—

seriously—

I don't care—

CLEM
I just feel like we're not on the same page.

FRANK
I don't like when people speak in cliches.

CLEM
I'm just being honest.

FRANK
I don't think honesty is one of your strong suits.

CLEM
No probably not.

FRANK
You're fucking killing me Clem.

CLEM
I don't think, on the list of the things that are killing you, I rank very highly.

FRANK
You'd be surprised.

CLEM
I don't like being idealized.

FRANK
I just like you.

CLEM
You like me because you idealize me.

FRANK
I thought you said I held you in contempt?

CLEM

    Where do you think the contempt comes from?

FRANK

    I'm in a terrible mood.

CLEM

    Should I just go?

FRANK

    No.

CLEM

    I feel like I should.

FRANK

    I can't tell if you're breaking up with me, that's all.

CLEM

    I'm telling you, I can't break up with you because we're not together. I'm just extricating myself from you.

Frank doesn't respond again.

CLEM

    I don't think you really know me; I want the record to state.

FRANK

    Does the idea of someone with substance caring about you make you feel uncomfortable?

CLEM

    Yes it does.

FRANK

    I've treated you so well.

CLEM

    I know you have.

FRANK

    So what gives?

CLEM

    I'd really like your blessing for friendship.

FRANK

    You have to have the courage to let things get ugly if that's the direction you're going to push them in.

CLEM
Forgive me, but I'm very weak.

FRANK
That's a shame.

CLEM
You're a delight Frank, really. I just don't know what you expected from me.

FRANK
Why do you keep talking about expectations?

CLEM
Because I feel all this pressure from you.

FRANK
What pressure? I haven't asked for anything except that you hang out with me when you're in town.

CLEM
No but you want me to redeem your life for you.

FRANK
That's just a thing you made up.

CLEM
No I can feel it very intensely.

FRANK
I just want a cool girlfriend who thinks I'm a cool boyfriend.

CLEM
For many reasons, I can almost be that, except not quite.

FRANK
That's not consoling.

CLEM
You're strong enough not to need consolation Frank; I really believe that.

FRANK
You may or may not be right about that.

CLEM
Look—I'm hot and smart and I wanna see other people, ok? I think that's normal for a girl my age.

FRANK
Totally.

CLEM
So let me go guilt free please.

FRANK

> The guilt is indigenous to the situation.

CLEM

> Well, that might actually be true—but not for the reasons you think—

FRANK

> Can we just spend the day together? Go to a park, drink a beer? Watch the sunset blah blah blah.

CLEM

> Happily, but I'm still gonna stay at my hotel tonight.

FRANK

> Why did you get a hotel?

CLEM

> My job is paying for it.

FRANK

> But why did you ask them to do that?

CLEM

> Because that way I have a place to go to.

FRANK

> But why do you want a place to go to?

CLEM

> We're spinning our wheels in the dirt.

FRANK

> I like the dirt.

CLEM

> I know you do.

FRANK

> Clem . . .

CLEM

> I'm so fond of you Frank.

Frank gets up to the fridge, gets a beer.

CLEM

> I'm not against the 'just for old time's sake' shag . . .

FRANK

> Just like old times? I saw you two weeks ago!

CLEM
  Ok, but it feels like old times.

FRANK
  Yeah! Because you're breaking up with me!

CLEM
  Extricating!

FRANK
  I don't care if you see other people; I don't care at all; I am not asking you to choose.

CLEM
  I'm asking me to choose.

FRANK
  Sounds lame.

CLEM
  It is lame, but that's just how things are with me.

FRANK
  This fucking sucks.

CLEM
  I know it sucks. I'm aware it sucks. I'm actively trying to limit the sucking.

FRANK
  That was oddly phrased.

CLEM
  Couldn't be helped.

FRANK
  Is there anything I could do differently?

CLEM
  Aside from being a completely different person? No.

FRANK
  Fucking hell.

CLEM
  Did that come off as mean? I was just trying to be clear.

FRANK
  You were plenty clear.

CLEM
  I think I just got caught up in something that doesn't feel very much like *me*—

FRANK

What's something?

CLEM

The lifestyle that you so beautifully and authentically represent.

FRANK

How would you describe that lifestyle?

CLEM

I can't fully describe it, but it has something to do with the death drive. You've read
Freud I'm sure—

FRANK

It's been a couple of decades, but sure.

CLEM

I'm just begging you to release me from the intense anxiety I'm undergoing in relation
to you.

FRANK

Oh Christ.

CLEM

Do you have a cigarette?

FRANK

On the bookcase, there's a pack.

CLEM

Frank that's wonderful news.

FRANK

Hand me one too?

CLEM

Of course.

They smoke in silence for a bit.

FRANK

So the death drive huh?

CLEM

I don't know what else to call it.

FRANK

Uhuh.

CLEM

It sounds like you basically agree with me though.

FRANK

> Well—one thing that people don't understand about me is how much goddamn pleasure I get out of life—

CLEM

> I think I sense that actually.

FRANK

> Clem. I love you.

CLEM

> You have to start weaning yourself off those feelings I think.

FRANK

> Clem.

CLEM

> Seriously.

FRANK

> I don't want anyone else; I just want you.

CLEM

> That's lovely, but.

FRANK

> But what?

CLEM

> I can't reciprocate—not in that way.

FRANK

> Ok.

CLEM

> Um.

FRANK

> Yeah.

CLEM

> I'm sorry.

FRANK

> Don't be?

CLEM

> Are you sure?

FRANK

> Yeah.

CLEM

You just never share anything about yourself, ever. I find it unsettling.

FRANK

Sorry.

CLEM

I'm just used to knowing more about the other person than they know about me.

More smoking and coffee-drinking in silence.

FRANK

Why don't we grab some beers and go to the park?

CLEM

I've already told you that I'm not opposed.

FRANK

Alright.

CLEM

Like now?

FRANK

Sure, might as well.

CLEM

Ok . . .

They start to get ready.

CLEM

Remember though—I have a hotel—

FRANK

I like hotel sex—

CLEM

Hope springs eternal.

FRANK

What else is it gonna do?

CLEM

Yeah, good point.

They exit.

Four

Maeve asleep on the couch.

Enter Adam.

He's clumsy. She wakes up.

ADAM
Shit, sorry to wake you up.

MAEVE
You're the roommate?

ADAM
Yup.

MAEVE
Sorry I'm in the way. I'm just crashing here for a few days; I hope Frank told you.

ADAM
Yeah yeah, it's fine. No worries. I'm just stopping by to get my shit. I have to catch a flight in a few hours.

MAEVE
Can I help or?

ADAM
No, it's fine, don't worry about it.

MAEVE
What time is it? I passed out.

ADAM
Uh it's like two in the morning.

MAEVE
Frank's not back yet?

ADAM
He disappears for days on end. I barely see the guy.

MAEVE
I feel bad I haven't hung out with him at all.

ADAM
He's hung up on this girl; it's fine.

MAEVE

He's a great guy, Frank.

ADAM

Yeah, good dude. I agree.

MAEVE

How do you know him?

ADAM

Oh you don't know the story?

MAEVE

I mean, I assumed like Craigslist.

ADAM

No—no—not Craiglist. Frank and I go way back.

MAEVE

To when?

ADAM

Wow Frank really doesn't let anything slip does he?

MAEVE

Uh no—what are you talking about?

ADAM

Oh—just—he and I used to work together; when I was coming up as a journalist, he was actually a photographer; we shared a bunch of big assignments.

MAEVE

Wait what?

ADAM

He's really never said anything?

MAEVE

No.

ADAM

It was another lifetime practically.

MAEVE

Whoa. It's crazy that he never said anything.

ADAM

I mean, that's Frank.

MAEVE

So you guys like reconnected as friends or what?

ADAM
    Yeah, I mean—I got divorced last year and moved back to Berlin—where I've lived off
    and on for a long time—and he was looking for a place, so it just kinda worked out.

MAEVE
    Do you have kids?

ADAM
    Yeah, a little girl back in the States.

MAEVE
    Oh wow. How old is she?

ADAM
    Four.

MAEVE
    Damn.

ADAM
    It was a have a kid to save the marriage kinda deal.

MAEVE
    Makes sense.

ADAM
    It made very little sense actually.

MAEVE
    Ah. Yeah. Um. I'm still wrapping my head around the fact that Frank was like a fucking
    war photographer.

ADAM
    For about a decade. He was a rockstar.

MAEVE
    What happened exactly?

ADAM
    Many things. It was war, you know? But there was one thing in particular.

MAEVE
    Oh?

ADAM
    The woman he was madly in love with was killed. A translator.

MAEVE
    Holy shit. Poor Frank.

ADAM

Funny thing was, I was in love with her too.

MAEVE

Did you like fight for this woman's affections?

ADAM

It was a bit like the movie Jules and Jim—do you know it?

MAEVE

No.

ADAM

Well then never mind.

MAEVE

I'm just beginning the phase of my life where I acquire culture, so.

ADAM

It's never too late as they say.

MAEVE

I've done vulgarity, now I want to do cultivation.

ADAM

Nice.

MAEVE

Dude—hold on—you're fucking with me—aren't you?

ADAM

Uh—it's a possibility, but one that I want you to explore for yourself.

MAEVE

Ok . . .

ADAM

You could always ask Frank if I'm bullshitting.

MAEVE

I'd rather drink bleach I think than ask Frank about his innermost heart.

ADAM

Actually, I think you'd take a certain amount of pleasure in making Frank emotionally dependent on you; I think you're very greedy in that sense, which is why I'm weary, but I digress.

MAEVE

If you're leaving, do you mind if I sleep in your room for the next day or two?

ADAM
>Yeah sure go for it.

MAEVE
>Thank you so much.

ADAM
>Don't kiss my ass; it's just a bed.

MAEVE
>This couch is killing my back to be honest.

ADAM
>It pulls out.

MAEVE
>Fuck, Frank didn't tell me that either.

ADAM
>His head was elsewhere I'm sure.

MAEVE
>Have we met before? You look so familiar.

ADAM
>I don't think so.

MAEVE
>Have you ever lived in New York?

ADAM
>A long time ago.

MAEVE
>How long ago?

ADAM
>Ten years ago.

MAEVE
>I was 13 and living in Florida.

ADAM
>So probably not then.

MAEVE
>You have a naturally familiar face then.

ADAM
>You might have seen it on a book jacket.

MAEVE

Maybe. People tell me I look familiar, but that's because they've seen me fuck.

ADAM

Oh right. I don't watch porn actually.

MAEVE

Good for you.

ADAM

I don't mean that in a pejorative way; it's just never something I've been into.

MAEVE

Honestly, I never watched porn before I started making it. I actually think porn is bad for people's brains.

ADAM

What's your favorite kind of scene?

MAEVE

I enjoy getting tied up and gagged and degraded—that kind of shit.

ADAM

Is that also what you like in bed when you're not shooting?

MAEVE

I think off-camera I prefer things a little more tender.

ADAM

Interesting.

MAEVE

Is it? Seems pretty standard perversion stuff.

ADAM

Sure, but it's still interesting.

MAEVE

You're just saying that because you think I'm cute.

ADAM

I do think you're cute, but I actually spent tonight fucking, so I don't think there's much I can do about it at this juncture.

MAEVE

That's fun. Who were you with?

ADAM

I went to a sex party with the woman I've been seeing, somewhat spontaneously—or entirely spontaneously.

MAEVE
Oh I would have gone. Too bad we didn't meet a day earlier.

ADAM
Yeah, too bad.

MAEVE
I also fucked someone tonight, but it wasn't very satisfying.

ADAM
Who?

MAEVE
A man I met at a club, who, as I found out later, turned out to be married. Highly regrettable.

ADAM
Uh. Uh. Yeah. My condolences.

MAEVE
What?

ADAM
Nothing. Never mind.

MAEVE
Ok . . .

ADAM
Anyway.

MAEVE
I always have such high expectations for Berlin nightlife, but it always seems to let me down.

ADAM
You can't bring a New York attitude to Berlin; you kind of have to let Berlin come to you.

MAEVE
That seems about right. I think I'm going to a rave tomorrow. Like I have to right? Like, those are the rules—

ADAM
Would it be ogreish of me to say the rave scene is not what it used to be?

MAEVE
That is pretty ogre-ish . . . yeah . . .

ADAM

I mean, look—it was just awesome back in the day. I was part of a loose group of like a hundred people or so—everyone knew everyone; several of us would DJ and there'd be parties organized every weekend—for years and years and years; it was a thousand year Reich of partying. It was truly like partying with your family. Apologies, this was not to become a rant. I just—I cannot convey how sanitized and giftwrapped a lot of the Berlin experienced is now—

MAEVE

Then why are you here?

ADAM

Because I'm a creature of habit and because this flat is cheap as fuck and because I own it.

MAEVE

That's awesome.

ADAM

It's ok. You're not doing porn anymore?

MAEVE

Not really. I'd like to try directing a la Frank.

ADAM

Do you like working with Frank?

MAEVE

He's one of the best people I've worked with; maybe the best—

ADAM

Nice . . .

MAEVE

Frank's erotic photography is actually amazing though. I hope he does more of that.

ADAM

Yeah he's talked about going in that direction exclusively.

MAEVE

I hope he does.

ADAM

We'll see.

MAEVE

What's your name? I realize I forget.

ADAM

Adam. You? I also forgot and was waiting for an opening.

MAEVE
>Maeve.

ADAM
>Right.

MAEVE
>What did he say about me? Anything?

ADAM
>Just that you were a friend of his. Nothing of note.

MAEVE
>Oh too bad. I feel like he secretly doesn't like me.

ADAM
>I see no evidence of that.

MAEVE
>The lack of evidence is the evidence.

ADAM
>Possibly.

MAEVE
>Do you have any drugs on you? I don't feel like going back to sleep.

ADAM
>I have a little bit of Molly. But is that really what you want right now?

MAEVE
>Not if you're not going to fuck me.

ADAM
>I could try to rally the troops I suppose.

MAEVE
>Do you expect pornstars to be slutty? I feel like I'm performing expectations out of sheer laziness and boredom.

ADAM
>I have no idea. It's not something I think about. How did you get into porn?

MAEVE
>That's such a trite question.

ADAM
>What do you expect? I'm a journalist.

MAEVE

I got into porn because I dropped out of school and I didn't wanna ask my dad for money. Trite question, trite answer. Next question?

ADAM

I'm too tired to have a next question.

MAEVE

Do you want to sleep? Don't let me distract you. Maybe I'll just go back out. I feel refreshed.

ADAM

Are you a manic type?

MAEVE

Obviously. If we were to fuck, how would you fuck me?

ADAM

How do you want to be fucked?

MAEVE

Hard then soft then hard again.

ADAM

Like a Pixies song—

MAEVE

Just like that.

ADAM

You seem like you'd be a really fun time.

MAEVE

I actually cry a lot and I'm very needy—don't let appearances deceive you.

ADAM

I'm aware of how women work.

MAEVE

Oh damn.

ADAM

Sue me.

MAEVE

What was the woman's name tonight that you went to the sex thing with?

ADAM

Monika.

MAEVE
She's German?

ADAM
Yup.

MAEVE
Are you into her?

ADAM
She's crazy, so yeah.

MAEVE
Like a lot into her or a little into her?

ADAM
Depends on my mood. Are you seeing anyone back home?

MAEVE
I was.

ADAM
But?

MAEVE
But I made some rash decisions and now I'm not seeing anyone.

ADAM
What rash decisions?

MAEVE
Let's just say that it involves betrayal.

ADAM
What did you fuck his best friend?

MAEVE
Uhhh—

ADAM
That's not very subtle.

MAEVE
I wasn't trying to be subtle.

ADAM
Clearly.

MAEVE
I filmed myself with the best friend and sent it to him—

ADAM

    Did the best friend know he was being filmed—?

MAEVE

    No—but I'm a pro—so—

ADAM

    Damn.

MAEVE

    Power move.

ADAM

    Is that power?

MAEVE

    No, it is the epitome of a power-less move.

ADAM

    Is it hard for pornstars to have relationships? Like stable, normal relationships? Like don't dudes get insecure—

MAEVE

    Sadly, yes and yes. I've never had a relationship stick for more than a few months.

ADAM

    And this last guy—I don't get it—you were trying to get out of it—or you wanted to stay but you sabotaged it? Sabotaged it right?

MAEVE

    Yeah. I wasn't used to things going well—so I felt out of control—so I created a situation where I had control.

ADAM

    Clever.

MAEVE

    Stupid.

ADAM

    Yes, also that.

MAEVE

    I'm honestly such a coward.

ADAM

    Aren't we all.

MAEVE

    I'd like to think there are a few exceptions out there.

ADAM

There are truly courageous people out there, but they're all dead naturally.

MAEVE

I mean, you're willing to risk your life for what you do—

ADAM

Is that courage or stupidity?

MAEVE

Classic question—

ADAM

Well, what do you think?

MAEVE

I think it's stupidly courageous.

ADAM

That's generous of you.

MAEVE

Does it make you feel good about yourself?

ADAM

Oh, very.

MAEVE

Figures.

ADAM

Why—do I come off as a huge narcissist?

MAEVE

You do, yeah.

ADAM

And do you think that's a front, or the real me?

MAEVE

I think it's a front for an even more self-absorbed self.

ADAM

I think you're right.

MAEVE

Last night, I went to some bar in Neukölln where everyone was dressed like an elf, or a duck-hunter, and there was a catboy there explaining how they'd cheated on their partner a dozen times. They said something that really resonated me: "The only thing that feels real is what's happening in the moment, and everything else feels unreal, so it's really hard for me to conceptualize consequences. I always just do whatever I want to do."

ADAM

Riveting.

MAEVE

One thing I'm learning is that everyone fills up their quota of pleasure and pain in different ways. Some are more extreme than others—but the results are the same—

ADAM

You should meet people who don't have limbs or faces.

MAEVE

I bet they're no more miserable than the rest of us.

ADAM

Like I said, you should meet them.

MAEVE

Are you sure you're not gonna rally? I'm getting really horny.

ADAM

I'm really feeling my age at the moment.

MAEVE

Do you want to be my spiritual father in that case then? I asked Frank but he wasn't game.

ADAM

I'm not into that either.

MAEVE

Shucks.

ADAM

Anyway, Maeve, it was nice chatting with you, but I really have to pack.

MAEVE

Aw, I'm having fun.

ADAM

Life isn't just about having fun, now is it?

MAEVE

This is my pouty face.

ADAM

I think you believe that saying yes to everything is cool and decadent, when in reality, the most decadent thing you can do is say 'no'—no no no no.

MAEVE

You don't wanna take the rest of the Molly and fuck?

ADAM

    Is that really what you want?

MAEVE

    Kinda.

ADAM

    I should just drink some water and sleep for a few hours and leave.

MAEVE

    Is that really what you want?

ADAM

    If I'm being completely transparent Maeve, in my mind, I've been fucking the shit out of you for the last twenty minutes—but I'm totally physically spent; I'd just embarrass myself.

MAEVE

    Alas.

ADAM

    Maybe I'll see you again.

MAEVE

    I doubt it.

ADAM

    Yeah.

MAEVE

    Missed connections are fun.

ADAM

    So are missed erections.

MAEVE

    Totally.

ADAM

    I think sometimes you recognize your own loneliness in someone and, in those moments, it's best to just turn and walk the other way . . . because there's no actual otherness—there's just sameness, and that's deeply redundant.

MAEVE

    I think so too, yeah.

ADAM

    So what's the deal? Are you going out? Are you going back to sleep?

MAEVE

Frank texted me that he's at a bar that I should come to.

ADAM

Alright, well, that sounds like a good game-plan.

MAEVE

Yeah, it does. Lemme just get properly dressed.

ADAM

Take your time.

Maeve gets herself ready to go.

Adam starts to pack, unenthusiastically.

MAEVE	ADAM
	(packing)
How does this dress look on me?	If you think about other peoples' suffering for long enough—to the point where you can actually feel it—you can begin to make sense of your own... but
Is it too revealing?	not until then. If your own suffering is purely abstract, purely a product of your own mind, not connected to anything else, then it's not only meaningless, but absurd. But once you do—once you have that wider sense of things—then you can begin to be a civilized person: a person with dignity.

MAEVE

It was nice meeting you.

ADAM

Yeah, for sure.

MAEVE

Goodnight. Safe travels.

ADAM

Yup. Goodnight.

Afterword

A playwright writes, but a play—the living, ineffable *thing*—is always something more than what was written, more than the playwright's intentions. I would be remiss then, in not acknowledging the powerful role that actors and audience, that directors and dramaturges, that time and circumstance have played in shaping these plays. On one hand, *Dimes Square, Quartet, Berlin Story*, and *Minotaur* have been authored, and on the other, they have evolved out of conversations, observations, rehearsals, performances. What makes them interesting— if they are interesting—is that, in their final form, they mark the collision between my own intentions and the polyvalent intentions of the world around me; they *are* the collision. The plays, mercifully, are more interesting, and better, than I am; they are more than their author because they may be interpreted and received in ways that I never thought of. My hope is that, in publication, these four plays may continue to surprise, and grow, even while remaining exactly the same.